A Handful of Stories

A Handful of Stories

Thirty-seven Stories by Deaf Storytellers

transliterated from the
Deaf Storytellers Video Tape Series

Roslyn Rosen, Ed.D., *Project Coordinator*
Bernard Bragg, *Program Coordinator*

Leonard G. Lane and Ivey B. Pittle, *Editors*

Gallaudet College, Washington, D.C.

The Deaf Storytellers Video Tape Series was sponsored by:

National Committee on Arts for the Handicapped
National Association of the Deaf
Gallaudet College Division of Public Services
Gallaudet College Pre-College Programs
Gallaudet College Special School of the Future
(with support from the W.K. Kellogg Foundation)

Published by Gallaudet College,
Kendall Green, Washington, D.C. 20002

Library of Congress Catalog Card Number 81-83444

ISBN 0-913580-77-5

Gallaudet College is an equal opportunity employer/educational institution. Programs and services offered by Gallaudet College receive substantial financial support from the U.S. Department of Education.

FOREWORD

A Handful of Stories is based on the Deaf Storytellers Video Tape Series, coordinated by Dr. Roslyn Rosen and Bernard Bragg. They were the guiding forces behind the transliteration of the signed stories into written stories. Bernard Bragg was responsible for recruiting the sixteen deaf individuals who participated in the Series. He also served as the video tape coordinator.

One basic objective of the Series was to promote an appreciation of deaf heritage. Thus, the signed and printed stories are based on the personal experiences of the storytellers or on information told to them by other deaf people. Viewers and readers of the stories will find them interesting, informative, sometimes incredible, occasionally moving, and often amusing.

The thirty-seven stories in the book are edited versions of the stories on the tapes. They are not exact duplications of the signed stories. The video tapes and the book may be used together, or they may be used independently.

Administrators, teachers, other professionals in educational and other types of institutions, deaf adults, and parents of deaf children will find a variety of uses for the nine video tapes. One person or a group of people may view them for entertainment and enjoyment. Students may look at certain stories to obtain bits of historical information. Teachers may incorporate the tapes as part of the course of instruction for sign language, English language, or reading classes.

The book may also be used for several other purposes. The stories may help to create interest, arouse curiosity, prompt thinking, or provide vicarious experiences for the readers. They can provide an excellent opportunity to encourage recreational reading. With some creativity and effort on the part of a teacher or leader, lists of words and their meanings can be prepared for some or all of the stories to build vocabulary. Questions and other types of exercises can be designed to develop understanding of the plot, important facts, and the moral of each story. Ideas or facts in the stories can be used as the basis for discussions to expand, reinforce, or review concepts. Some specific suggestions for follow-up activities are included at the end of the book.

Although the tapes and the book can be useful learning tools, it is the hope of those who participated in this Series that one of the greatest benefits derived from their use will be that of sheer enjoyment which comes from viewing the tapes or reading the book for personal pleasure!

For more information about the Deaf Storytellers Video Tape Series, write to Gallaudet College Library, Media Distribution, 800 Florida Avenue NE, Washington, DC 20002.

CONTENTS

MEET
THE
STORYTELLERS

Bernard Bragg

If Bernard Bragg is no mean whiz at telling a good story, that is because he has never been known to be dull. In addition to his accomplishments as a storyteller, he is a well-known actor, mime, director, teacher, playwright, and TV personality. He is a graduate of Gallaudet College, and he has studied with Marcel Marceau, the internationally known mime.

As an actor Mr. Bragg has starred in such recent hits as *And Your Name Is Jonah* and *The White Hawk*. As a mime he has originated many famous routines; as a director and playwright he has directed and coauthored the recently acclaimed play, *Tales from a Clubroom*, and the comedy, *That Makes Two of Us*. His past achievements include appearing in a weekly TV show, "The Quiet Man," which was produced by KQED in San Francisco; being a cofounder of the National Theatre of the Deaf; and serving as a good-will ambassador of the United States Department of State.

This born raconteur livens up his stories with such flair that he always casts a spell over his audiences.

Edward E. Corbett, Jr.

Ed Corbett, a native of Shreveport, Louisiana, began his professional career as a graphic arts teacher at the Louisiana State School for the Deaf. Since leaving his home state, Dr. Corbett has been actively involved in programs and services that benefit the deaf community. He received his B.A. from Gallaudet College and his M.A. from the California State University at Northridge. He was the first deaf recipient of a Ph.D. from Gallaudet College.

Dr. Corbett has had an impressive career in deaf education. In addition to his years as a teacher, he served as the communication-community education coordinator at the Margaret S. Sterck School for the Hearing Impaired in Newark, Delaware; the assistant superintendent at the Maryland School for the Deaf at the Frederick and Columbia campuses; and an intern with the U.S. House of Representatives' Committee on Education and Labor, where he monitored compliance with Section 504 of the Rehabilitation Act of 1973 and helped draft the Interpreter Training Act, a part of Public Law 95-602. Dr. Corbett is currently the director of the National Academy of Gallaudet College. He has several publications to his credit, including the recently published *Teachers of the Deaf: Descriptive Profiles*, which he co-authored with Dr. Carl J. Jensema.

Florence B. Crammatte

Widely known as an organizer and innovator, Florence B. Crammatte is currently the co-chairperson, with her husband, of the fundraising campaign to restore Gallaudet's 19th-century gymnasium for use as the Alumni House. As national president of Phi Kappa Zeta sorority (1960-67), she established its biannual newsletter, *The Phi Kappa Zetan,* and the ØKZ Woman of the Year Award. Her other literary efforts include editing Rev. Guilbert C. Braddock's book, *Notable Deaf Persons,* and editing a monthly newsletter for an employees' association.

Flo's first employment after graduation from Gallaudet College was as a museum assistant with the Hispanic Society of America in New York City. She taught for a short time at the Louisiana School for the Deaf and entered federal civil service during World War II. Her longest position was with the Plant Industry Station, U.S. Department of Agriculture, as a statistical assistant. Upon retirement from USDA in 1972, she worked part-time in the Office of Alumni and Public Relations, Gallaudet College. She is now retired again but continues to do volunteer work.

Flo has been an active member of the Gallaudet College Alumni Association. She served as the first chairperson of the GCAA's Laurent Clerc Cultural Fund Committee (1967-1973). Under her guidance, the LCCF committee has made many contributions to the Gallaudet campus, including the presentation of a bronze cast of the original small model of the Daniel Chester French statue of Thomas Hopkins Gallaudet and Alice Cogswell, and the provision of seed money for numerous cultural projects.

Gilbert Eastman

Gilbert Eastman, a graduate of Gallaudet College, has long been associated with theatre at Gallaudet College. After he earned his master's degree in drama from Catholic University, he was instrumental in starting the drama department at Gallaudet College. Gil Eastman was a founding member of the National Theatre of the Deaf, and it was there he received much of his professional theatre training. After leaving NTD, he returned to Gallaudet College, where he developed two courses, *Sign Language Translation for the Theatre* and *Visual Gestural Communication as a Sign Language Base* (formerly *Nonverbal Communication*). He has traveled both nationally and internationally to conduct workshops in Visual Gestural Communication. He has written and produced (at Gallaudet College) two plays, *Sign Me Alice* (published) and *Laurent Clerc: A Profile*. Mr. Eastman has conducted extensive research on Laurent Clerc, who was the first, and possibly, the most important deaf teacher in the United States. His research and subsequent play have led him to lecture about Laurent Clerc at numerous sites. Mr. Eastman is currently a professor of theatre and chairman of the Theatre Arts Department at Gallaudet College. He resides in Crofton, Maryland, with his wife and two daughters.

Jack R. Gannon

Jack R. Gannon, director of Alumni and Public Relations at Gallaudet College, was born November 23, 1936, in West Plains, Missouri. He became deaf at the age of eight as a result of spinal meningitis, entered the Missouri School for the Deaf in 1946, and graduated in 1954. From 1954-1959 he was a student at Gallaudet College, majoring in education, and devoting a great deal of his spare time to his two loves: football and journalism. As editor of the college newspaper, *The Buff and Blue*, he won first class ratings for the paper from the Associated Collegiate Press. He co-captained the varsity football squad in 1957, was president of the Alpha Sigma Pi fraternity, and served as editor of the 1959 *Tower Clock*, the college yearbook.

Following graduation from Gallaudet, Mr. Gannon was an instructor in graphic arts and a coach at the Nebraska School for the Deaf. In 1967 he was honored as "Coach of the Year" by Omaha's WOW-TV when his eight-man football team had an undefeated season.

Jack Gannon returned to Gallaudet College in 1968 to serve as director of Alumni Relations. In 1971, when the alumni and public information offices were reorganized and combined into the new Office of Alumni and Public Relations, Mr. Gannon became director of that overall operation. This office is responsible for the alumni program, publications, public relations, the new national information center, and the college visitors program.

Mr. Gannon is the author of *Deaf Heritage: A Narrative History of Deaf America*, recently published by the National Association of the Deaf.

Mr. Gannon is married to the former Rosalyn Lee of Winston-Salem. They live in Silver Spring, Maryland, with their two children, Jeff and Christy.

Jerald M. Jordan

Jerald M. Jordan is a 1948 graduate of Gallaudet College. He has been with the college for twenty-one years in various capacities — as an instructor in physics and in mathematics, as founder and first director of the computer center, and currently as director of Admissions and Records.

Mr. Jordan's interests are many and varied. In addition to his work as a human guinea pig for the U.S. Navy, which he describes in his story, he has obtained a private pilot's license, flown solo as far west as Wichita, Kansas, and as far north as Detroit, Michigan. His current interests lie in boating on the Chesapeake Bay.

"JJ," as he is known, is also president of the International Committee of Sports for the Deaf, which oversees the Deaf Olympics. In this role he and his wife, Shirley, have traveled widely throughout Europe, Japan, and South America.

Barbara Kannapell

Barbara Kannapell sees herself as a person first, and a deaf person second, through her work as an advocate with Deafpride, Inc. She is the president and co-founder of this community-based organization in Washington, D.C., which advocates human rights among deaf people and their families, and promotes bilingual education for deaf children. Barbara was born into a deaf family—her parents, uncle, and two aunts are all deaf. Her sister is the only hearing member of the family. She is a niece of the famous George Gordon Kannapell, who was well-known in the deaf community for his humorous antics at NAD rallies in the 1950s. She got many good stories from her deaf relatives.

Barbara travels widely as a lecturer on various topics ranging from advocacy to bilingual education for deaf children. All these topics draw more from her life experiences than from books. She worked as a research assistant at Gallaudet for seventeen years following her graduation from Gallaudet. She earned a master's degree in educational technology from Catholic University, and she is currently a Ph.D. candidate in sociolinguistics at Georgetown University. She is presently working as a linguistics specialist with the Instructional Development and Evaluation Center at Gallaudet.

Eric Malzkuhn

Eric Malzkuhn, better known as "Malz," fell in love with sign language at the age of twelve, and it proved no passing fancy. He is still caressing signs into outlandish and charming configurations as a drama teacher at the Model Secondary School for the Deaf (MSSD), some 40-odd years later. His first blockbuster was *The Jabberwock,* loosed upon an unsuspecting world when he was seventeen.

Malz taught in Michigan and California. He has also been a printer, advertising copywriter, and vocational rehabilitation field agent. He earned a master's degree in drama from Catholic University. He was the first director to stage a full-fledged musical in sign language—*Oliver*—in 1976 at MSSD. He has worked with interpreters all over the nation and has taught artistic-theatrical sign language in many colleges via workshops and at the National Theatre of the Deaf's summer school program.

Malz's wife, Mary (a Gallaudet political science professor), is studying for her Ph.D., and Malz is eagerly anticipating receiving the first letter addressed to "Dr. and Mr. Malzkuhn." Malz and Mary have four boys; one is their dog and one is a deaf son (he's a teacher in California—the son, not the dog). Malz continues his antics on the stage, but his favorite role as an actor was Ben Franklin in *1776.*

Thomas A. Mayes

Tom Mayes has lived and worked in many parts of the United States, attended seven different universities, and was mainstreamed in the public schools some 40 years before 94-142 became a law. Presently he is vice president of the Division of Public Services at Gallaudet College.

Dr. Mayes became deaf from spinal meningitis at the age of six. He attended the Oregon School for the Deaf for several years before entering the public schools of Baker, Oregon. Except for three years in the fields of journalism and advertising in Chicago, he has spent his entire professional career in the field of education, much of it with the C. S. Mott Foundation in Flint, Michigan. He was on the faculty of California State University at Northridge before coming to Gallaudet. He holds a bachelor's degree from the University of Chicago and a Ph.D. from Michigan State.

Mary Beth Miller

Mary Beth Miller is a well-known figure in theatre productions for the deaf. She became an actress after graduating from Gallaudet College. She is the daughter of deaf parents, and she has a deaf sister.

Mary Beth has been involved in many interesting projects. She co-authored *Handtalk, An ABC Book of Sign Language and Fingerspelling;* she has been involved in the production of "Rainbow's End," a television series for deaf children and their families; and she is currently active in forming the New York Deaf Theatre in New York City. She will serve as an actress, writer, and director for this group. In addition to her work in theatre and television, Mary Beth has also been active in education of the deaf. She holds two master's degrees, one in educational theatre and one in deaf education.

Ray S. Parks, Jr.

Considered a "Renaissance" man by many who have known him, Ray S. Parks, Jr., in part, owes his multifaceted experiences and achievements to his admiration for Leonardo da Vinci. He has been recognized for his athletic feats in many sports—he won five consecutive A.A.U. diving championships in Virginia and was a participant in the 1961 and 1965 International Games of the Deaf. He won a bronze medal in high-board diving and a silver medal in wrestling.

Mr. Parks is also known for his talents as an actor (he was once with the National Theatre of the Deaf) and an educator. He has presented numerous workshops and lectures in the areas of communication, theatre arts, education of the deaf, and curriculum development; his services continue to be in demand.

A 1960 Gallaudet College graduate, he has begun studies toward his doctorate degree in educational administration at New York University, and he is also currently an educational director at a school for the deaf.

Nancy Rarus

Nancy Rarus has long been an active member of the deaf community. Her involvement extends to both social and educational realms. The deaf daughter of deaf parents, and the mother of deaf children, Ms. Rarus has an intrinsic appreciation of the deaf culture. She has spent many years working at improving the quality of life for deaf citizens.

While teaching at the American School for the Deaf, in West Hartford, Connecticut, she was active at both the state and national levels of the NAD; she was coordinator of the In-Service Total Communication Program for the junior high school at the American School; and she established and coordinated the Sign Language Instructor's Pool of Connecticut (SLIP). In addition, Ms. Rarus has served on the National Captioning Institute Advisory Board.

Ms. Rarus now makes her home in Arizona, where she continues to be active in the deaf community. Her most recent appointment has been as Chairlady of the Community Outreach Program of the Deaf Administrative Advisory Board in Tucson, Arizona.

Michael Schwartz

Michael Schwartz, deaf since birth, grew up in New Rochelle, New York, where he attended the public schools. He received a B.A. in English from Brandeis University, graduating cum laude (with honors). He then obtained a master's degree in theatre from Northwestern University and taught drama at the North Carolina School for the Deaf in Morganton.

Mr. Schwartz has also been a member of the troupe of the National Theatre of the Deaf. After a year of touring the United States with the company, Michael decided that the law offered tremendous tools to aid in the struggle for deaf people's rights, and so he went into hibernation for three years at New York University. He graduated in 1981 from the NYU School of Law with a J.D. degree. He has great hopes for the future and seeks to devote his legal skills to the deaf community.

James M. Searls

James M. Searls, known as "Matt," is a graduate of Gallaudet College with bachelor and master of arts degrees in social work and counseling, respectively. While he was a student at the Virginia School for the Deaf and the Blind, he participated in dramatics, an activity he continued throughout his college years and into the present.

Mr. Searls is a deaf son of hearing parents, brother of deaf and hearing siblings, and husband of a deaf elementary school teacher. During his four years at the Counseling and Placement Center at Gallaudet, he acquired considerable knowledge and skills in career and personal counseling. He is currently the director of the Preparatory Studies program at Gallaudet. Mr. Searls and his wife, Susan, make their home in Cheverly, Maryland.

Deborah M. Sonnenstrahl

Deborah M. Sonnenstrahl, who now serves as director of the Fine Arts in Education program at Gallaudet College, considers herself to be a "late bloomer." Being a late bloomer, however, has its advantages. One gets to appreciate and cherish the finer points in life much longer.

It was at Gallaudet College that Debbie's life began to blossom. Up to that time she had lived in a relatively tame world, learning to read and speak. When she enrolled at Gallaudet, it was against her own wishes! However, her parents foresaw the advantages of her getting an education on an equal footing with her peers, rather than fighting the hassles in a hearing college. While at Gallaudet College she learned the beauty of sign language, and then there was no stopping her. She grew from a wallflower to a ham on stage, gaining a reputation as an actress, instructor of art history, and an advocate of deaf rights, especially in the area of museums. She later graduated from Catholic University with a master's degree in art history. With her varied interests, she has never lost her sense of beauty.

In her present job Debbie has done much to further the cause of making museums accessible to the deaf. She has been the recipient of many honors and awards, including the Teacher of the Year award, the Tower Clock award, dedication of the Gallaudet yearbook to her, and "Best Overall Performance by an Actor or Actress" in the Maryland One-Act Play Tournament, in which she competed against hearing actors. She makes her home in the shadow of the Smithsonian Institution complex in Washington, D.C.

Frank R. Turk

Frank Turk is probably one of the most readily recognizable figures to deaf high school students and young adults in the country today. He has spent his entire professional career actively involved in helping young deaf people become aware of their capabilities and realize their fullest potential.

Frank, a native of Hibbing, Minnesota, became deaf at the age of four from spinal meningitis. He attended the Minnesota School for the Deaf, where he was an active participant in school activities. His participation in school activities, especially sports, continued throughout his college years at Gallaudet College. After graduating from Gallaudet in 1952, Frank became a counselor and the director of extracurricular activities at Kendall School. Between 1965 and 1980 he served as the director of Junior NAD. In this role he traveled across the country, speaking to groups of young deaf people. During these "talks" Frank always stressed the need for deaf youth to develop self-discipline, self-respect, and self-confidence.

Frank is currently the acting director for the Office of Student Life at Gallaudet College, but he still maintains that his first and foremost commitment will always be to the deaf youth of America.

1

My First Summer Job

Bernard Bragg

There is a story I would like to share with you. I remember it well, so well that it seems like it happened yesterday. Really, it happened many years ago when I was a young student at Gallaudet College.

I went home to New York for the summer after my first year in college. I spent the whole month of June looking for a job. It was difficult to get a job because so many young people were looking for work. It was a frustrating experience for me. Every time I went into an office and applied for a job, I was told, "No. Sorry, we don't have any openings."

One morning I noticed an advertisement in the newspaper for a dishwasher at a summer camp. I read the ad and thought, "That's fine. I can be a dishwasher." I was excited as I went to the office on 42nd Street near Fifth Avenue. I found that I was the first applicant to arrive. I filled out the application form and then waited. Finally, the secretary told me I could go in for an interview. I went in and found a man standing there. It was obvious that he was the boss. I handed him my application form. He read through it and then started to talk to me.

I had to explain to him that I was deaf. I said, "Wait; I can't hear; please talk slowly." He looked at me and said, "What?" I told him again I was deaf, and he said, "Oh." He pointed to a door and told me to go through that door. I followed his instructions. I opened the door and walked through it, closing it behind me. I found that I was in the hallway near the elevator where I had just come up. I was shocked! He had rejected me without any explanation. I got into the elevator, and as it descended, I felt very letdown. I couldn't understand why he didn't give me a chance to explain that I could do the job well. It didn't require hearing!

I went outside. There were a lot of people passing by on the side-walk, hurrying along, bumping into me as they walked. The hot sun made me sweat as I walked along. After walking a few steps, I stopped. I thought, "If I give up this easily, I don't think I can go very far in life. I'd better go back and try again." I turned around and went back in the building. I wrote some notes as I rode the elevator. The notes were for the boss. When I walked in, the secre-tary tried to stop me, but I went right on, walked in, and gave the notes to the boss. He took them and pointed to the door. I told him I wouldn't leave until he read the notes. He looked at me with exas-peration, and then started glancing through my notes. He became interested in what I had written. I had explained that I was a student at Gallaudet College, that I needed a job, and that dishwashing didn't require hearing. As he could see, I had arms and they were strong. He kept on reading; he seemed surprised that I could write. Finally, he asked me to have a seat. I sat down, and he asked me if I could lipread. I told him I could a little. We talked awhile, and I got the job.

I'll never forget the day I arrived at the summer camp in Massa-chusetts. It was a beautiful place, set in a clearing surrounded by trees. The scene was exhilarating, but I had to go in and start wash-ing a stack of dirty dishes. (To tell the truth, I hate to wash dishes, but I had to earn a living.) For the next month, I worked like a horse as a dishwasher. But relief finally came.

One day the camp director asked for volunteers to help a nearby farmer with hay gathering. I volunteered because I wanted to get away from the kitchen. Early the next morning, I joined the group of farmers and started pitching hay onto a wagon. I worked very hard that morning, so hard that I had blisters all over my hands. My hands were really sore, but I kept on pitching hay until it was time for lunch.

After lunch I was tired, so I decided to lie down under a tree and rest. When I woke up, I found myself all alone. Everyone had gone back to work. I was late! I ran, got my pitchfork, and rushed to the wagon. The foreman was standing on top of the hay. He looked at me with his hands stretched out, nodding his head up and down. Then he put his hands over his ears and stuck out his tongue at me. I was stunned. My first thought was to turn around and walk away, but I decided to stay and keep working. I began pitching hay onto the wagon again. The hay piled up on the wagon as we moved down the field. It got higher and higher. At the same time black clouds began appearing all around us. It looked like it was going to rain at any moment. We hurried to get all the hay we could on the wagon, take it to the barn, and put it in the barn before the rain came. We worked like crazy.

When we got to the barn, the foreman excused everyone except one of the farmers and me. He told me to go up in the loft and spread the hay out while the two of them pitched it up into the loft. The two men pitched the hay in so fast that I couldn't spread it out fast enough. Dust swirled around me; I could hardly breathe; I started coughing; but they kept pitching the hay, and I kept spreading it. I could see that the foreman enjoyed making things hard for me. However, I knew that I could not last much longer. Just as I was about to give up, the foreman looked at me and said, "All right, you can change places with me." He went up in the loft, and I stepped outside. The cold air brushed against my face, and I felt refreshed again. I picked up the pitchfork; now it was my turn. I began to pitch hay into the loft faster than he could spread it. He soon became surrounded by hay, but I kept on working until all the hay was in the loft.

Just then lightning flashed, thunder rolled, and the rain poured down. I staggered off the platform and hit the ground. Rain splattered me as I lay there and rested. After a few minutes I got up, wiped the rain off my face, and began to leave. I noticed the foreman standing under the eaves of the barn, smoking. He nodded his head, indicating he wanted me to come over. I went to him, and he put his hand on my shoulder. I felt as if I had been made a knight— it was like he had tapped me on the shoulder with a sword. I saluted and then turned and walked away.

Trapped!

Deborah M. Sonnenstrahl

W hen I was a student at George Washington University, in Washington, D.C., I took a course on American Art. One day my teacher gave us some homework. He wanted us to do research on previous artistic styles. My topic was silent movies up until 1929. My teacher wanted me to focus on these movies; they had captions, but no soundtrack. I suspected he did this because of my deafness.

I began looking for information, but I couldn't find anything. I went to my teacher and asked, "Where can I find some good materials for my research?" He suggested that I go to the John F. Kennedy Center for the Performing Arts. He told me that the American Film Institute, located in the Kennedy Center, had an excellent library. I would find a lot of information there about the history of the movies.

I walked into the Kennedy Center one day and asked the woman at the desk where I could find the American Film Institute.

She said, "Go around that corner, and you will see an elevator. Take the elevator to the third floor. You will find the films, books, and papers there."

I thanked her and walked to the elevator. I was so excited I could hardly wait to begin my research. I rang the bell for the elevator and waited. Finally the door opened and I walked in. I was alone in the elevator.

For some strange reason I got a funny feeling; I did not know why. I had never been afraid to be in elevators before, but that time I was. I pushed the funny feeling aside and said to myself, "Debbie, just be cool." The elevator went up and stopped on the third floor, but the door did not open. I started to perspire, and my heart started pounding faster and faster. I pushed the third floor button; I pushed it again and again, but nothing happened! I tried to pry the door open, but I couldn't. I used all my strength, but nothing happened, nothing at all. Then, I thought of pushing the button for another floor. I pressed a button and the elevator went down. The door opened on the first floor, and I ran out. I yelled for the woman at the desk. I cried, "The door wouldn't open on the third floor. The elevator door was shut and I couldn't open it. I couldn't do anything."

The woman looked at me. She said, "But lady, the door on the third floor opens in back of you."

"In back of me? You mean on the other side?" I asked.

"Yes," she said, "on the other side."

Oh, just imagine it! How many people must have looked in from the other side and seen me!

The Eavesdropper

Jack R. Gannon

I work in the Alumni Office at Gallaudet College in Washington, D.C. One day I needed to call Bernard Bragg, a deaf actor, at the National Theatre of the Deaf in Connecticut. I asked my secretary to please call him. We have a good telephone interpreting system in our office. I pick up the phone and talk into it, and the secretary listens and tells me what the other person says. It works fine.

That day we called and got the National Theatre. I spoke with a woman, saying, "Hello. My name is Jack Gannon. I would like to talk with Mr. Bernard Bragg, please."

The woman said, "Oh, I'm sorry, but Mr. Bragg is deaf."

I was surprised because I thought the National Theatre would have an interpreter for him. "Oh, that's all right," I said, "I'm deaf, too."

"What?" the woman said. "You're deaf. But . . . but . . . you understand me?"

I replied, "Yes, sure, I'm following every word you are saying."
Wondering, she asked, "How?"
I answered, "Oh, I have an eavesdropper next to me."
And she said, "Ohhh. . . ."

POW!

Michael Schwartz

When I was a small boy, I went to summer camp every year. One summer I went with my older brother who was about nine years old. We were with a group of hearing boys from New York City. All of them were tough kids from Harlem and the Lower East Side. They played rough with me and with each other.

One of the boys was named Jon. I remember him well. Jon looked exactly like one of the characters on the TV show "The Addams Family." He had a short haircut and curled-up nostrils. For some reason, I didn't feel good about him. One day Jon came to me and moved his mouth like he was talking. I didn't know sign language at that time; I was oral. I looked at him and asked. "What did you say?" He just moved his mouth the same way. Then, I realized he was making fun of me, of the way I talked. I became embarrassed and flustered. I didn't know what to do, so I walked away.

The same thing happened every day. Jon would come to me and make that same mouth movement. It embarrassed me, but it also made me angry. I felt . . . well, I didn't know how to feel. I decided to find my brother. He was older and wiser, perhaps he would know what to do. I found my brother and told him about Jon. I asked him how I could make Jon stop embarrassing me in front of other people at the camp. I was crying a little bit because I was so upset. I didn't know what to do. My brother looked at me. He made one gesture and said, "Punch him." My brother was busy, he couldn't talk with me, so he just gave me that one line—"punch him"—and left.

I thought, "Punch Jon? I couldn't do that; I couldn't hit another person." I didn't like to fight, and besides I was afraid. But I remembered my brother's one line, "Punch him." One day I went in to my bunk, my bed happened to be right next to Jon's bed. No one else was there, so I went in and got a book. When I turned around, Jon was behind me. He was doing the same thing, making fun of me! I looked at him and then punched him! I hit him right in the mouth. It happened so fast that I didn't know what I was doing. Jon hit the floor; he was out cold. I thought, "My God, what have I done?"

I looked at Jon and he was shaking. Then he began waking up. He looked up at me and was so scared that he took off. I put my book under my arm and walked outside. I was shaking by that time, but I had a good feeling inside of me. It was a beautiful day, and I enjoyed myself, walking around the camp. About an hour later, I saw Jon again. I didn't want to fight him, but I didn't have to. When he saw me, he took off again. He didn't want to get close to me. From that day on, I walked very proudly!

My Horse and I

Mary Beth Miller

When I was a very young girl, I liked to sit and dream and imagine things. One day I fantasized that I had a horse. He was black with a white spot on his forehead. The spot looked like a star. He was a beautiful, big horse, and how he could gallop! I thought about my horse often. I talked to him, played with him, petted him, and rode him. I loved my horse, he was smart. He could jump far without hurting himself. The horse of my fantasy was very real.

One day I went to visit my mother's friend. (She is deaf, too.) I told her, "I have a horse at home. He eats grass. He is black with a white star on his forehead. Last night I rode and rode him."

My mother's friend said, "How nice."

The next week I went to visit her again. I told her some more about my black horse with the white star. I told her how the horse jumped and how I rode him all over the farm.

My friend said, "How nice."

Every week I would tell my friend different stories about my horse. But finally, my stories ran out. My mind was blank; I didn't know what to do. One day I said to her, "I don't have my horse anymore. He died."

"Your horse died!" she said. "What happened?"

"Oh, my uncle shot him," I answered. "It was my uncle's fault."

My friend felt bad, but she wasn't really sure about my story. Later, when I wasn't around, she went to my house, knocked on the door, and said to my mother, "Do you have a horse, a black horse with a white star on his forehead?"

"What are you talking about?" my mother asked. "We don't have a horse here. The city doesn't allow horses; it is against the law."

My friend, puzzled and wondering, went home.

The next day I went to my friend's house again. "I buried my horse," I told her. "I put a cross on the grave. I prayed and I cried."

My friend said, "Are you telling me the truth?"

"Yes," I replied, "I'm telling you the truth."

"No, you are not," she said. "I asked your mother, and she said there's no black horse with a white star. She was surprised. You are telling me a lie."

"I wasn't telling you a lie. I was only fantasizing, but my horse seemed real to me."

2

Spaced Out!

Jerald M. Jordan

I would like to tell you a story about a deaf man and some experiments with weightlessness and motion sickness. The man was not Superman, but perhaps we could call him Super J.J. I am that man.

Early in the 1960s, a group of U.S. Navy doctors were looking for a cure for motion sickness. They wanted to prevent people from becoming sick while they were on boats or while they were weightless in space. A lot of people have a tendency to become ill and throw up when they are on a boat or a rollercoaster. Many hearing people have this problem, and many deaf people have it, too. I don't because when I was seven years old, I had spinal meningitis. That disease destroyed my hearing and my sense of balance. From that time on, I have had no sense of balance, and I have to depend on my vision for balance. If I stand on one leg, I can balance fine; but if I close my eyes, I fall down.

The doctors knew that I had no sense of balance, and they wanted to compare me with people who get motion sickness. A few other deaf people and I went to a naval base in Florida for some experiments. Many of the experiments were the same as the ones they did on the astronauts before they went into space. The doctors were hoping to lessen the effect of weightlessness on hearing people.

Some of the experiments were really boring, but some of them were exciting. The most exciting experiment of all took place in a large four-engine airplane. Inside there were no seats; everything had been taken out and soft padding had been used to cover the inside of the plane. In the weightless experiment if someone hit the padded wall, ceiling, or floor of the airplane, the person wasn't injured. The doctors took movies and pictures so they could study what happened.

When the plane was in the air, it started out flying level; then it went up into an arch. While the plane was in the arch, we deaf people were weightless for about forty-five seconds. We were very heavy for a brief time, but then we began to have no weight. All we needed to do was touch something and we floated. We rolled over, forward, backward, to the side—everywhere in the air—with no support. We couldn't push against or touch anything hard because we would hit the wall and bounce back and forth. It was difficult to stop; someone had to catch us and stop us from bouncing. It is hard to describe exactly how I felt during that experiment, but it was wonderful.

One of the hearing doctors with us was a short man who weighed about 250 pounds. Once when we were weightless, I picked him up! I tossed him through the air like a football to another person who caught him and threw him back to me. It was easy, and the doctor was a good sport!

However, every good thing ends. When the plane came down from the arch, we felt that we weighed more than twice our normal weight. That was because of the pull of gravity. At the time of the experiments I was rather fat; I weighed about 190 pounds. At two-and-a-half times my weight, I felt that I weighed about 500 pounds. After a while I felt my normal weight again. Then the cycle was repeated—flying level, going up into an arch, and coming down from the arch. During each arch of the plane, we became weightless and floated in the plane.

Some of the hearing people didn't like the experiments. Once we went up with a group of hearing sailors. A few of them were navy pilots who had flown jets for many years. When we took off and became weightless, one of the sailors thought it was easy. But he soon got sick and began vomiting. He became so sick that the doctor on the plane had to help him. The sailor was cold and shaking.

Because of this, the pilot had to dump most of the fuel to lighten the plane and then land. The sick sailor was taken to the hospital. It was strange that he, a hearing person, got sick, but I never did. I had a good time with the experiments.

Another interesting experience was when a group of hearing sailors and a group of deaf people went to Nova Scotia. We were there in February, and that is one of the worst places in the world in the winter. It was extremely cold, we had to wear warm clothes — hats, mittens, the works. Usually the water off Nova Scotia is very rough, but the day we were to board the ship to begin our experiment, the water was calm. The navy people weren't too happy because they wanted rough water. We waited three days for some bad weather, but there was none. Finally, on the fourth day a storm hit. It was so bad that three ships went down in the ocean that day. We were told to hurry and get ready to board the ship.

Before we left the calm water in the harbor, the doctors took a blood sample from each person in the experiment. They wanted to do that every hour so they could analyze what happened to the body and how it changed while we were on the rough water. After the doctors took blood samples we sailed out into the ocean, and the full force of the storm hit us! The water was rough and the waves were high — thirty to thirty-five feet high! The ship went up and down, and I tell you, I was scared. I couldn't walk; I had to crawl on all fours. After about an hour of this, though, I lost my fear and became rather confident that the ship wouldn't sink.

The doctors wanted to take blood every hour, so after the first hour I went to one of their offices. There the doctor was, laid out sick. I went to another doctor, and found the same thing. All the doctors were so ill they couldn't conduct their experiment. The hearing sailors were sick, too. The six of us who were deaf and one hearing person were the only ones not in bed. We sat around a table playing cards; there was nothing else to do. It was dark outside, and the ocean was rough. I looked at the hearing person and said, "You're not sick?"

"No, I feel fine," he answered.

"Why aren't you sick?" I asked him. "Everyone else is sick."

He replied, "I have spent thirty-five years on a U.S. destroyer. Destroyers are rather small ships which are easily tossed about."

We continued playing cards. About fifteen minutes later I looked and the hearing man was gone, too. That left only the deaf people, plus, thank God, the captain of the ship and his crew. They had sailed these waters for many years and the rough seas didn't bother them.

The crew members were French. They were hearing people, but they didn't speak English. That night, while we were playing cards, the captain came to the table. He looked at us and gestured to ask if we were sick. We gestured back that we were fine. He couldn't believe it. We continued playing cards all night; we couldn't sleep because we would have fallen out of bed. From time to time the captain came in and asked us if we were ill. He seemed almost disappointed when we answered that we were not. I didn't understand why he seemed disappointed. Later I found out that the admiral, a navy doctor who was responsible for the experiment, had made a bet with the captain. He bet a case of Scotch whiskey that we would not get sick. That was why the captain hoped to see us sick, but he lost the bet!

So you see, that is how some deaf people helped our astronauts before they ever went to the moon. Without our help, maybe they would never have gotten there because of problems with weightlessness and motion sickness. Thank goodness for the help of some deaf people in getting the astronauts to the moon!

Gallaudet Theatre on Broadway

Eric Malzkuhn

I would like to take you back in the past—back to a time when my waist was smaller and I had a lot more hair. That was in the 1940s when I was a student at Gallaudet College. I was fascinated with the theatre and wanted to become involved in it. Naturally, I volunteered to act. My first "role" in a play was as the curtain-puller. That was all I did. However, I began to get some acting roles after that.

The summer I was a sophomore I read many different plays. I was looking for a good play for Gallaudet to put on the next year. I wanted something better than Samuel French's *Blue Plate Special*. I wanted something new, something exciting, so I read and read. Then something hit me! *Arsenic and Old Lace* was the play I wanted! I knew it was being acted on Broadway at the time. I was young and inexperienced so I was not afraid to write and ask to see if we could get the play. I sent a letter to the Dramatist Play Service, which controlled the rights to *Arsenic and Old Lace*. I received a letter saying that they were sorry, but the play was not available for amateurs until the end of the New York run. Also, it was not available to professional groups without an agreement about money and other matters. I was heartbroken, but I wasn't satisfied either. I wrote another letter, a longer one, explaining that the Gallaudet students were not professionals, but they were not amateurs, either. I told them that all the money earned was put into the treasury for costumes, sets, and similar things for play productions. I also said that we were the best sign language actors in the world! I sent the letter. I waited one week, but there was no response. I started to get depressed. Then one morning word came to me that there was a box downstairs for me. A box? I went down and found a box from New York for me. My eyes opened wide, and my heart began beating fast as I looked in the box. There were twenty-one scripts of *Arsenic and Old Lace* and a note. The note said, "Is this what you wanted?" It was signed by Howard Lindsay and Russell Crouse. Maybe those names are not familiar now, but they were famous people in 1940. They wrote *Life with Father*, and they produced *Arsenic and Old Lace*.

When I got the box, the Gallaudet actors were ready to do the play on the small stage in Chapel Hall. We were satisfied with that. I was to direct the play; oh, I was so excited. Our group met and began to make plans. While we were planning, a boy came and said there was a telegram for me. "Who would send me a telegram?" I wondered. I got it, opened it, and read, "Why not forget about presenting *Arsenic and Old Lace* in Chapel Hall? Why not do it at the National Theatre in downtown Washington?" Wow! I couldn't believe it. Then I noticed that the telegram said in March. Our rehearsal time really wouldn't be long enough if we did it in March. May was the best time; March was too soon.

I didn't know what to do, but before I had a chance to do anything, another telegram came. I opened it. "Forget the first telegram," it read. "We realize we were pushing you. Plan on performing the play on Broadway in May."

I was floating on air! I decided I couldn't direct the play; I was only nineteen. I had better give the job to someone wiser and more skilled than I. I ran to Dr. Hughes and asked him, "Would you like to direct our play?"

"Well," he said, "I am rather busy right now."

"How would you like to take our play to Broadway?" I asked.

"Broadway!" he said as his eyes popped out.

I explained, and he accepted the offer. We shook hands on it.

We got a letter two or three days later from the Broadway producers. "We would appreciate it if you and Dr. Hughes would come to New York, watch our play, meet our actors, and talk about various plans," they wrote. Lindsay and Crouse thought this visit would be important for publicity for Gallaudet College and also for their play. So we went to New York. They made hotel reservations for us and told us just to sign for our meals at the hotel. This was a new experience in my life! The first time we went to eat, I ordered lots of things. After the meal, I very nonchalantly asked for the check and signed my name. The waiter looked at it. He looked at the name and then looked at me. He had never heard of Eric Malzkuhn. The waiter went to phone about the check while I sat there. When he came back, he was all smiles. Everything was fine.

That night we went to the Fulton Theatre, now called the Helen Hayes Theatre, and saw the play *Arsenic and Old Lace* for the first time. We sat in the third row of the center section. The curtain opened and Boris Karloff, the star, came on stage. Chills ran up and down my spine. Karloff is the famous actor who played Frankenstein in the movies. I'll never forget that moment; it was very exciting. During intermission, at the end of the first act, Russell Crouse came down the aisle and waved to us. He asked, "Is everything all right?"

"Fine," we replied. People looked at us wondering who we were. My buttons were popping, but I couldn't help it, I felt so proud. When the play was finished, we met Boris Karloff. He was very pleasant, very nice. He shook my hand. "I am happy to have you come here," he said. "You can use my costume and my shoes." That night we met in the hotel and talked business.

When it was time to order drinks, they asked me if I wanted a drink. "Well," I thought, "I'm not in college right now." Drinking was forbidden at Gallaudet, but I was in New York. So I decided I would have an old-fashioned. Then they asked Dr. Hughes.

He looked at me and said, "I'll just have some milk, please." Lindsay said, "Oh, no. Malz won't tell on you."

"Okay," said Dr. Hughes, "I'll have a whiskey sour."

We were really stuck on one point. We hadn't gotten approval from the Gallaudet administration to do the play in New York. Imagine, if you can, that we had to go to the president of Gallaudet and ask him to let us know within three days if our group could go to New York to do *Arsenic and Old Lace*. We met with President Hall and explained the whole thing. Dr. Hall, a man I loved very dearly, said, "No. I am sorry, but you can't. I am rejecting the idea."

We were heartbroken. He never explained his reason. Perhaps he feared that the deaf being linked with Frankenstein (Karloff) would create some sort of monster-image on people's minds. Or possibly he didn't want to change the play into a silent one. I don't know his reason, but he turned it down.

We thought about it and tried to decide what we could do. Then Jon Hall, the president's son, said, "Ask the faculty for a vote." Jon was a very good friend of ours. He worked hard for us; he helped us a lot with the sets. We went to the faculty and they voted that we should do the play on Broadway.

We did it! We went to New York, and we were a big hit. It was fantastic! Dr. Hall admitted in front of a national audience that he was wrong. The play, which was also filmed, was a great success. We were in New York for five days. We stayed at a hotel and signed for our meals like Dr. Hughes and I had done before. We rehearsed all day, but at night we went to see plays. We saw Gertrude Lawrence, Victor Mature, and Danny Kaye in *Lady in the Dark* and Theresa Wright in *Life with Father*. It was magnificent, marvelous. Once a newspaper man came in and asked for a picture of me scaring Karloff. Can you imagine me scaring him? I tried and the man took the picture of me with my features frozen in a grimace, trying to scare Boris Karloff!

During the time we were rehearsing the play, I wore Boris Karloff's costume. I wore it when I was out walking, and when I went out for lunch. I even wore his shoes. He called them his lucky shoes because he wore them inside his boots while playing the part of Frankenstein. When I first tried the shoes on, he asked if they fit. They were too big, but I said they were fine. I put some paper in the toes of the shoes.

On May 10, 1942, the curtain opened on *Arsenic and Old Lace* performed by Gallaudet students on Broadway. One man, a rather famous deaf priest, was sitting on the aisle. He told me he was afraid that deaf people gesturing and signing would be too much like overacting and people would laugh at us. He sat on the aisle so he could leave quickly. Well, he didn't leave. He sat in rapt attention, just as the critics did. Afterward the priest said it was marvelous. Burns Mantle, probably the most famous New York critic at the time, said that he thought Gallaudet students should come back to New York every year. That did not happen, but that is another story.

Those moments were some of the most beautiful of my life. Of course, being on Broadway, I became very conceited. When I went back to Gallaudet, I still had a big head. I was strutting about, and Elizabeth Peet, one of our professors, came up to me and said, "Mr. Malzkuhn, it was a wonderful, wonderful play. But your French is not so wonderful." That helped reduce my swelled head and got me back to normal again!

Man's Best Friend

J. Matt Searls

A long time ago two boys lived in the country near a small town. One boy's name was John. The other boy, who lived a few houses down the lane, was named Mark. John and Mark were the best of friends.

One day John and Mark had been playing. When they got tired, Mark said, "Maybe we could walk into town." John said he really didn't want to do that. "What else do we have to do?" asked Mark. "Maybe we can buy some candy and look around." So John agreed to go.

As they walked toward town, they noticed a man putting up a sign. John and Mark were curious, so they watched the man until he finished, and then they walked over and read the sign. It said that a circus was coming to town the next week. John said, "Maybe we can go to the circus." Mark agreed it was a good idea, but they didn't have any money.

They saw on the sign that a ticket to get into the circus would be one dollar. Where could they get the money? Mark had an idea. He said, "We could sell lemonade this week for five cents a glass and earn a dollar each. Then we could buy our tickets for the circus." John thought that was a good idea. All that week the two of them sold lemonade to the passersby at five cents a drink. They worked hard in the hot sun. As the time drew near for the circus to open, they counted their money. They counted out two dollars for the tickets, but there was some money left. They counted it and found there was another dollar. They had earned three dollars altogether. John suggested that they use the extra money to buy popcorn, cotton candy, and other things like that at the circus. So they divided the dollar, fifty cents each, and waited for the circus to open.

That morning John got up, dressed quickly, ate no breakfast, and took off to Mark's house. When Mark was ready, the boys left his house. In the distance they saw the Big Top. They ran toward the tent, and soon there it was before them—the Big Top!

The boys looked around; they had never seen anything like the circus. They bought their tickets and went inside. When they got inside, they saw the trapeze, the high wire, the bright colors, and the beautiful lights. They saw the animals—elephants, lions, dogs, and other animals. John said that the circus was going to be exciting. They bought some candy and then looked for a seat right down in front. They sat down and soon the ringmaster came in. Then the circus began. One act was the lion tamer and the lions. When that was over, the bears, elephants, horses, and other animals performed. Then it was time for the man on the high wire. Mark was excited, but John was nervous; he was afraid to watch the high wire act. Mark thought John was chicken. After that the dogs came out—big dogs, fat dogs, cute little dogs with bows, many kinds of dogs. John was fascinated. The dogs jumped up, they sat, they lay down, and they rolled over. Too soon the circus was over, but both boys had enjoyed it.

On the way home Mark asked John, "What act did you enjoy the most?"

John said, "I liked the dogs; they were so intelligent."

"I liked the man on the high wire," Mark said. "That took some courage."

As they walked along, John thought he noticed something across the road. He asked Mark if he saw something, but Mark said that he didn't see anything. John suggested they check it out. They did and found a cute brown puppy with a white spot on his forehead. He was cold and cowering, and his ears were drooping. John thought the puppy looked afraid. What should they do? Should they leave the puppy there or take him home? John decided to take him home. Mark thought it was better to leave him there. If the puppy was lost, his mother might find him. But John felt that if the puppy were left, he might die of hunger.

John picked up the little dog and said good-bye to Mark. When John got home, he knocked on the door. His mother opened the door and saw the puppy he was holding. She said, "You put that dog back." John told his mother that the little dog was hungry and cold. With his droopy ears, the puppy looked so sad. John's mother said, "You can bring him in, but if you do, you have to bathe and feed him. Tomorrow you must put an ad in the newspaper about the little dog. Maybe someone owns him."

John was a little depressed about the ad, but he agreed. He went to the newspapers the next day and explained to them how he found the puppy. There were advertisements in the papers for a week trying to find the owner. All that week John took care of the little dog. What a change! The puppy became quite healthy; his eyes sparkled and his ears perked up. At the end of the week John had heard nothing. It seemed that no one wanted the dog. John's mother said he could keep the dog. However, John had to promise to feed him properly, take him outside to go to the bathroom, and accept all responsibility for the dog. John agreed.

John had to decide what to name the dog. Since the dog had a white spot on his forehead, maybe his name should be Star. That name didn't sound too good to John. Perhaps Spot would be a good name. That was the name John decided on for his dog. John and Spot became inseparable. John trained his dog to sit, lie down, and roll over.

John spent so much time training Spot that Mark became jealous. Mark said, "John, you are always playing with your dog." John reminded Mark that he had to train Spot and take care of him; it was his responsibility. Mark told John that the two of them were always together before. Now the dog was interfering, and he didn't like it! He suggested that John get rid of Spot. John said, "I love the dog. It can be the three of us; we can all be friends."

Mark replied, "No, the three of us can't be friends. I can't be friends with Spot."

"Wait," said John. "I'll show you." Then he looked at Spot and said, "Friends," and the dog extended his paw to Mark.

But Mark said, "I don't want to touch the dog; he is dirty."

When the time came for John to go to school, his mother said, "John, you have to leave the dog at home. When you come home from school, you can play with him." John was sad; he wanted to take Spot to school. However, John went to school, and then every evening when he came home, he took care of his dog and played with him. John also played with his friend Mark. When the school year ended and summertime came, John and Mark were still friends. Mark continued to feel that Spot was interfering with his and John's relationship. Mark would say to John, "Leave the dog at home and let's go out."

John would always say, "No. He's a good dog; he is our friend."

"He is not my friend," Mark would reply. But John always took Spot with them. The boys went swimming and did different things, but the dog was always with them.

One summer day John and Mark decided they would go swimming in a pond near a big waterfall. They liked going there; they used to swing from a rope tied to a tall tree and jump into the water. As usual, Mark wanted John to leave the dog at home. "Spot can't swim," Mark said. "He can't jump from the rope. Why should he go?"

John said, "Maybe Spot can look around and even go for a swim."

Mark didn't say any more, but he was angry.

The three of them walked to the waterfall and pond. It was a beautiful place. John and Mark jumped from the rope, fell into the pond, swam, and played all afternoon. Meanwhile, Spot sniffed around and watched the two boys. When the boys grew tired, they lay on a rock and enjoyed the hot sun and the cool breeze. Soon John and Mark were asleep.

A little later, Mark woke John up and asked, "Would you like to go for another swim?"

"No," John said, "I'm too tired. I am going to lie here in the sun. You go on for a swim if you want to."

Mark got up to go, but he told John he didn't want Spot to go with him. John told Spot to stay there. Then John fell asleep again; it was very comfortable in the hot sun.

A little while later Spot began to bark. John woke up and saw Spot looking down at the water at the bottom of the waterfall. Mark was down there; he had obviously fallen and was trying to swim. John and Spot ran down the hill. They both jumped in the water, and John pulled Mark to safety. When they were on the bank, the two boys breathed a sigh of relief. John asked what had happened. Mark explained that he had fallen from the rope and sprained his ankle; now it was swollen.

"Mark," John said, "Spot barked and woke me up. It is a good thing that the two of us were here to help you."

Mark replied, "Yes, I guess you are right." He looked at Spot who sat there wagging his tail. Mark said, "Friend," and Spot extended his paw. Mark shook Spot's paw and then put his arm around John. From that day on, John, Mark, and Spot were friends; the three of them were always together!

Have Interpreter, Will Talk

Edward E. Corbett, Jr.

I want to tell you a true story—something funny that really happened to me. When I was working with the United States Congress in Washington, D.C., I worked with the Committee on Education and Labor. One of my duties was to study Section 504 actions on the federal level. The 504 law says that handicapped people will not be discriminated against or prevented from participating in programs or activities that require federal funding. In doing my job, I contacted many different departments such as Health, Education, and Welfare; Defense; Labor; Justice; State; Agriculture; and others.

At the Department of Health, Education, and Welfare (HEW), I wanted to get in touch with someone in the Office of Civil Rights, OCR for short. I wanted to find out from that person what problems OCR had involving Section 504. I needed information about problems such as how many people complained about discrimination under 504, what actions had been taken by that office regarding the complaints, and how the complaints had been or could be resolved.

Through an interpreter I made a phone call, well actually not one, but more than twenty calls, with no success. Finally after two weeks, I talked with a member of Congress. I explained to him that my phone calls had not been returned and that I could not get through to the Office of Civil Rights. He called the Secretary of HEW, who had a secretary call the director of OCR. The director asked someone to call me to set up an appointment so we could get together. Finally the phone call came.

I was at the Maryland School for the Deaf when the call came from the Office of Civil Rights. The man who called said that their office understood I had been trying to set up a meeting at OCR, and they were ready to meet with me. The call came on Thursday, and the gentleman suggested that we get together the following week on Monday, Tuesday, or Wednesday. I said that was fine; Monday would be best for me. We set the meeting for Monday afternoon at two o'clock, and I wrote it on my calendar. Then the man asked me if I would bring along an interpreter. I said, "No! Section 504 says that you should provide me with an interpreter. Why should I always have to look around and find an interpreter to take with me to different meetings? Why should I suffer?" For these reasons I did not agree to bring an interpreter.

"Well," the gentleman said, "perhaps we have a problem."

I agreed, "Yes, we do. Today is Thursday, and we only have Friday, Saturday, Sunday, and Monday to find an interpreter. It is not easy to get an interpreter on such short notice. Sometimes you have to reserve one as much as a month ahead of time.

"But that is okay," I continued. "We can forget about an interpreter because we can still communicate."

"How?" he asked.

"We can write notes."

"That is impossible," the man replied.

I got very angry and said, "I can read and write!"

"No, no, don't misunderstand me," he said. "I said it is impossible because, you see, I am blind. I can't read or communicate through reading."

I started to laugh. I was with the United States Congress, and I wanted to discuss something really important about 504 with someone at the national level. He was blind, and I was deaf! I laughed and laughed, and he laughed and laughed. It was really funny. We postponed the meeting to another time when we could get an interpreter.

Later I related my strange experience to a few members of Congress. They said they didn't realize that interpreters were hard to find. They thought perhaps something should be done to help provide more interpreters. I agreed and said we should come up with a way to set up interpreter training programs. "If we could find some money," I suggested, "we could find many hearing people and could teach them to become interpreters."

The members agreed with me. So, we took that idea and wrote a bill for Congress. That bill became the law which President Carter signed in 1978. It is called the Interpreter Training Act of 1978.

3

Laurent Clerc:
The Greatest Teacher of All Time

Gilbert C. Eastman

June 28, 1864, was an important day for deaf people. On that day many people gathered in a church in Washington, D.C. The big event was the birth of Gallaudet College. The president of the college was only twenty-nine years old. His name was Edward Miner Gallaudet. He stood up, saw all the people gathered in front of him, and gave his opening inaugural speech. Government officials, members of Congress, ministers, and deaf children from Kendall School were seated on the platform to watch this great celebration.

Several members of Edward M. Gallaudet's family were in the audience that day, including his sixty-six year old mother, Sophia Fowler Gallaudet, and his oldest brother, Thomas Gallaudet. Thomas and Edward were the sons of Thomas Hopkins Gallaudet, the founder of the first permanent school for the deaf in America. Now Thomas Hopkins Gallaudet's youngest son was helping to establish Gallaudet College. A deaf man was also sitting there, an artist, whose name was John Carlin. He was to receive an honorary degree. Several famous speakers came up to the podium, one by one, and gave long speeches. Then, Edward Miner Gallaudet introduced an old man who was seventy-nine years old. The old man trembled a little and appeared to be weak. When Gallaudet fingerspelled his name, Laurent Clerc got up, walked to the podium, and faced all of the people. The hearing people applauded, and the deaf people waved their handkerchiefs, as was their custom. Clerc looked at Edward Miner Gallaudet, who was so young. He looked at Edward's older brother and at their mother. Even though he was old, Clerc's mind was still very clear and straight, and he began to think back many, many years. . . .

Laurent Clerc was born in France in 1785. Those were terrible times in that country—it was the time of the French Revolution, Bastille Day, and a reign of terror during which many people, including the king and queen, were beheaded. Blood flowed all over France. It was at that time that Clerc was born.

Clerc was born in LaBalme, a town in the south of France. At the age of two he had an unfortunate accident. He was sitting in a high chair and, somehow, the chair fell over on the hearth. Laurent hit the side of his head. As a result of the fall, he became deaf and he lost his sense of smell. Clerc's sign is made by brushing the first two fingers on the cheek because of the two scars he had on the side of his head.

Young Clerc played with the children in the neighborhood for several years, but when they went to school, he was left alone. He played by himself outside—in the woods, beside the streams, and on the rolling hills—until he was twelve years old. That year his uncle came to visit the family. He saw that Laurent was already twelve years old and had never been to school; he had no formal education. The uncle persuaded Clerc's parents to send him to Paris, where they had a school for the deaf. His mother and father hated to send their son so far away from home. However, they permitted his uncle to take him in a stagecoach from LaBalme to Paris.

Clerc's uncle dropped him off at the school; there he met a deaf teacher named Jean Massieu. The superintendent of the school, Abbé Sicard, was not there at the time. Abbé Sicard had been arrested, put into jail, and was waiting to be beheaded. Jean Massieu was so worried about the superintendent that he decided to call the deaf people of Paris together. He wanted to see what they could do to get the Abbé released. The people decided to sign a petition and take it to the French Assembly. There, in front of all the hearing people, Jean Massieu read the letter from the deaf people pleading that Abbé Sicard be released. After several days on consideration the Assembly decided to free the Abbé and let him return to his school, the Paris Institute for the Deaf.[1]

While Clerc was growing up at the school, be became Abbé Sicard's favorite pupil. The Abbé and Massieu both taught Laurent. He proved to be very brilliant even though he hadn't had any schooling until the age of twelve. Later, when Clerc was in his twenties, Abbé Sicard offered him a teaching position at the Institute in Paris, and he accepted.[2] Clerc taught in the Paris school for many years.

People from other countries visited the school to see Massieu's and Clerc's classes and to study how they taught deaf children. Their techniques began to spread to other countries. A man from St. Petersburg, Russia, came to the school to see Clerc's work. He was impressed and asked Clerc if he would be willing to teach in Russia. Clerc agreed to go; he was excited and eager to teach in a Russian school. The Abbé did not like the idea, but he said it was Clerc's decision. The Russian returned to St. Petersburg to make arrangements. Clerc waited and waited for the Russian to return, but he didn't come back. Finally, Laurent heard from him; he said that they didn't have enough money, so he had to cancel the offer of a teaching job. Clerc was disappointed, but if the man from Russia had found some money and taken Clerc to St. Petersburg to teach, this story would be quite different.

Napoleon had many enemies in France, one of whom was Abbé Sicard. Sicard was afraid of Napoleon, so he decided to go into

---

[1]One summer my wife and I went to Europe. We stopped in Paris and visited the Paris Institute for the Deaf. We looked around the very old buildings, which are still in use by the school. We met some French children and adults who were deaf; it was a nice experience for us.

[2]I have a picture of Clerc as a young man in Paris. I found the picture, a very small photograph, in the Library of Congress and had it enlarged. In the picture the front of Clerc's head is bald. As I looked at the picture, I wondered why the front of his head was bald, since later pictures of Clerc show him with a full head of hair. I found the answer to my question. Clerc was a young man during the time of Napolean, the French emperor, At that time the young men in Paris looked to Napolean as their fashion guide. Napolean was balding in the front, so many of the men then shaved the front of their heads. Later on, of course, Clerc let his hair grow in front.

exile. He took Clerc and Massieu, and they escaped across the channel to London, England. While in England, the three teachers continued their work; they traveled around and gave lectures to the English people. They went to lecture halls where many of the important people gathered. The people asked questions which Sicard interpreted to Clerc and Massieu. The two deaf teachers answered the questions by writing on the blackboard. The hearing people were shocked that deaf people could write.

One day the Duke of Kent, the Duchess of Wellington, and the Duke of Orleans, three very important people in England, were at the lecture. The Duke of Wellington, the Duchess' husband, was leading the English army against Napolean's troops at Waterloo. During the lecture, while the people were asking questions, Sicard was interpreting, and Clerc and Massieu were answering, the Prince Regent came rushing into the lecture hall. "The war is over," he shouted! "We have won at Waterloo, we defeated Napoleon." Napoleon lost, the Duke of Wellington (whose wife was sitting there that day) and his men won, and Massieu and Clerc witnessed that historical event.

Abbé Sicard made plans for Clerc, Massieu, and himself to leave London and go back home. They continued to give lectures up until their last day in England. A short man from America attended their last lecture. The man was very impressed with the lecture and the question and answer session. When the three teachers were finished, the young man from America came to the front and introduced himself to Sicard, Clerc, and Massieu. His name was Thomas Hopkins Gallaudet. Gallaudet shook hands with the three men and then explained that he wanted to establish a school for the deaf in America. Sicard invited Gallaudet to go to Paris and visit his school; however, Gallaudet wanted to spend a few more days in England. He traveled around, observing the various methods of teaching deaf children used in English schools. Gallaudet became quite frustrated with what he saw. After he finished his travels in England, he went to Paris to learn the art of teaching the deaf. He studied Massieu's and Clerc's classes for several months.

Meanwhile, the people in Hartford, Connecticut, who had sent Gallaudet to Europe, were saying to him, "Come home. You have stayed too long." Gallaudet realized it was time to leave, so he told Clerc, "I have to go back to America. Could you find two deaf teachers for me who are skilled both in English and French?"

Clerc said he would be happy to help. He found two deaf teachers and presented their names to Gallaudet.

Gallaudet looked at the names and changed his mind. He said to Clerc, "I don't want these men; I want you."

"You want me?" Clerc replied. "But, I don't know English."

Gallaudet said, "You can learn English."

Suddenly Clerc became excited about the idea of going to America. Gallaudet offered him a three-year contract and Clerc accepted. Of course, Sicard became very upset; he didn't want Clerc to leave Paris. The deaf children there needed him. Massieu didn't want him to go; he thought it was a stupid idea. But Clerc was stubborn and decided to go anyway.

Before leaving for America, Clerc wanted to go home to visit his mother and the rest of his family. Clerc's mother had already heard the news and she was upset. She asked, "Why are you going to America?"

"I must," Clerc said. "I must help the deaf children in America. They have no teachers. There are no hearing or deaf teachers in America."

His mother tried to persuade him to stay in France, but Clerc remained firm. After two weeks his family finally gave up and wished him good-bye. He took a stagecoach back to Paris. The day after he arrived in Paris he went to the office and signed his three-year contract. Everything was ready. He packed his suitcase and went by coach to Le Havre to board a ship. Clerc stood on the dock and looked out across the sea. What was ahead for him was unknown, but he mustered up his courage and got on the ship.

Traveling by ship from France to America in those days took fifty-two days. Gallaudet and Clerc used their time wisely during the trip. Gallaudet taught Clerc English, and Clerc taught Gallaudet sign language. You might think the trip was a pleasant one, but it was not. They encountered terrible storms at sea. People got sick, and many passengers had to stay in bed. Clerc suffered a lot during the trip. Sometimes the sea was calm, so the ship remained under the hot sun for several days. The room where Clerc stayed would get very, very hot, and he would perspire. When the weather changed, the room would get very, very cold, so Clerc would pile on the blankets. But Gallaudet continued studying sign language, and Clerc continued studying English until they reached New York.

When the ship arrived in New York, Clerc looked around the city. New York City didn't look like it does today! Clerc didn't like the looks of the buildings. The city seemed very plain and humble compared to Paris which had fancy buildings, museums, and theatres. Clerc became homesick for Paris; he wanted to go back, even after the long trip. But he agreed to go on with Gallaudet, so they traveled by stagecoach to Hartford. Clerc again became upset because the people there all dressed the same.

Gallaudet and Clerc went to the Cogswell house in Hartford. They met Mrs. Cogswell, who immediately asked someone to go call her daughter Alice. The two men talked with Mrs. Cogswell while they waited for Alice. Clerc was still disappointed with America and kept saying he wanted to go home. Gallaudet, who was interpreting for Clerc, was heartbroken that the teacher did not like America. Finally Alice Cogswell, who was deaf, came in and met Clerc. She began to gesture and sign to him. Clerc was shocked! Alice already knew some sign language. She used some gestures, but she also used signs. Clerc wondered how she knew them. He asked and found out that Gallaudet had been teaching Alice before he decided to go to Europe. Since Gallaudet didn't want to leave Alice at home without a teacher, he put her in a private school for girls. The teacher at the school, Lydia Huntley, taught Alice and all the hearing girls in the class to use signs so Alice and the other girls could communicate. Thanks to Lydia Huntley, the girls developed their own sign language. When Clerc saw this, he thought it was wonderful. Alice and Clerc became very close.

Gallaudet wanted to establish a school for the deaf in Hartford. He worked for one year to raise money. Then he established his school, not in a school building but in a hotel.[3] The school took over the first, second, and third floors of the hotel. The classrooms were on the first floor and the sleeping quarters on the second and third floors. When the school opened, there were seven deaf pupils; one

---

[3]I have a picture of that hotel. While I was doing my research, I knew that the American School for the Deaf had a picture of three of the early buildings, but they had no picture of the original building. I looked around and by accident, I found a very tiny picture. The name on it was City Hotel; I had heard that name before. I learned that the City Hotel was the exact place where Gallaudet and Clerc established the first school. I was so excited. I took the picture to a photographer and had it enlarged.

of them was Alice Cogswell. The school stayed in the hotel for a year until Gallaudet, with the help of some businessmen, found another place, a big house. They moved into the house, and it became the first real school building, although it was the second building for the school.

Clerc taught the seven students in the school. The two oldest pupils were Elizabeth Boardman and Sophia Fowler. These two girls were between seventeen and nineteen years old. The other students were about fourteen. For two years, while Clerc taught, he kept noticing Elizabeth. Gradually he fell in love with her. He proposed marriage to her, and they were married after she finished school. After the birth of their first baby, Clerc decided to go to Philadelphia with his family. The school there needed some help. Clerc helped the school make some changes to improve its program. He also taught in the school for a time. While the Clerc family was in Philadelphia, Clerc heard that the famous American painter, William Peale, lived in the city. Clerc asked the painter if he would paint a portrait of the Clerc family. Mr. Peale agreed, and he painted two pictures for them.

After seven months in Philadelphia, Clerc and his family moved back to Hartford. The family gradually grew larger. Laurent and Elizabeth had six children, four girls and two boys. Two children died at birth. The oldest daughter became a teacher at the school for the deaf, the second child became a minister, their other daughter married the mayor of Hartford, and their youngest son studied the silk business in France. After several years he came back to the United States and established his own business in New York City.

As Gallaudet and Clerc worked together, their friendship grew even stronger. Together they taught, raised money, and conducted experiments. Some of their experiments were strange! Gallaudet was not satisfied with the manual alphabet. He was still a strong oralist and was not happy with fingerspelling. He invented a new alphabet—the alphabet of scents. (That is puzzling, isn't it?) He took twenty-six jars and put a different substance in each jar. Each substance had a strong odor. For instance, A was ammonia; B was bergamot, which smells almost like mint; C was cinnamon; and so forth. Gallaudet put the twenty-six different scents on one side of a wall. A student would like a stick, dip it in the jar, and wave it over the top of the wall. Students on the other side of the wall would smell the scent and know which letter it was. For example, the students would smell the odors for the letters *h-e-l-l-o* and thus communicate through the sense of smell. Gallaudet thought this was wonderful, but it seems to have failed, mainly because Clerc couldn't use it; he had lost his sense of smell when he was two.

Gallaudet still wasn't satisfied with fingerspelling, so he decided to try another experiment. He invented the alphabet of facial expressions. It used facial expressions for each letter. *A* was for awesome; *B* for boldness; *C* for curiosity; *D* for despair; *E* for eagerness; *F* for fear; *G* for gladness; and so forth. Can you imagine trying to spell through facial expressions and trying to understand what was being communicated? There are stories, though, about people using the alphabet of faces. Here is an example:

> Many, many years ago, two deaf adults traveled together on a stagecoach from one town to another. They sat next to each other. Two hearing people sat across from them. The deaf passengers did not want to sign, so instead, they talked to each other with their facial expressions during the trip. The hearing people across from them kept trying to figure out what they were doing. (The reaction was similar to when you talk with your hands on a bus and the other passengers stare at you.)

Gallaudet and Clerc tried to find the best teaching methods while they worked together. After thirteen years at the school, Gallaudet decided to resign. Clerc chose to stay in America. He went back to visit his family and friends in France from time to time, but he ended up staying in the United States for forty-two years. Including his eight years of teaching in Paris, Clerc taught deaf children for fifty years. He devoted his full attention to helping deaf children. He never went to college; he had no time for himself. However, three colleges presented him with honorary degrees.

Clerc's mind came back to the present. There he was standing before all the people at the opening of Gallaudet College on June 28, 1864. He thought how wonderful it was to take part in the event. He began his speech and thanked the people for inviting him to see this most important day. It was a great honor for him. He spoke briefly. When he finished, the people applauded and the deaf people waved their handkerchiefs, again.

Laurent Clerc remained a Frenchman at heart even though he lived in America for many years. He was French, but people thought and spoke of him as an American. Deaf people call him "The Father of the American Instructors of the Deaf." When Clerc passed away in 1869, people contributed money to a memorial fund. Eventually, there was enough money to get a bust of Clerc made. The inscription on the bust says, "The Apostle of the Deaf Mutes of the New World." This line was taken from a letter written by Abbé Sicard to Clerc just before Clerc left for America. In his letter the Abbé said, "You are the apostle of the deaf mutes of the New World."

I must tell you that Clerc really is the greatest deaf teacher of all time!

CHAPTER

4

Me or We*

Frank R. Turk

I want to talk to you young people about attitude. I have traveled to many schools for the deaf and have seen some students with good attitudes and some with bad attitudes. What is attitude? Some people think they know, but they really can't define it. I can tell you an easy trick on how to remember the meaning of attitude.

Attitude is divided into three areas: first, how you feel; second, how you act; and third, how you think. An adult many years ago impressed upon me that attitude is something you cannot take for granted. You can't get *fat* on attitude. The key word is fat. *F* is for how you feel; *A* is for how you act; and *T* is for how you think. F-A-T! If you take a quiz and your teacher asks you the meaning of attitude, you can answer it, "Attitude is how you feel, how you act, and how you think." You will probably get an *A* for that. Then I want you to write a letter of thanks to me for my help!

One thing I would like to change in young people is the *me* attitude. Young people who always ask, "What's in it for me?" have the *me* attitude. They don't understand the importance of having a *we* attitude. A *me* attitude is so-so, but a *we* attitude is fine. Maybe

---

*This story is in the form of a lecture.

you know someone with a *me* attitude, and you want to forget that person. No, you should keep that person in your life or or in your group because he or she may have several important leadership traits. For example, that person may be an aggressive person. That's important. Many leaders, like Lyndon B. Johnson (LBJ) and John F. Kennedy (JFK), were successful because of their aggressive attitudes. Maybe you can help the aggressive person in your life or group. Work with him or her to change the *me* to a *we* attitude. Then the person will understand the importance of serving the group.

Another thing to emphasize is a positive attitude. For example, on TV you find weather reports on four or five channels. Your favorite may be Channel 5, another person's may be Channel 7, but my favorite is Channel 9. Why? The weather reporter on Channel 9 is very positive. He never uses the words *partly cloudy*. Instead he uses *partly sunny*. The words *partly cloudy* and *partly sunny* have the same meaning, but sunny is more pleasant, more positive. Partly cloudy sounds more negative.

Once, during my school days in Minnesota, I had a glass of water in my hand. An adult saw me with the glass in my hand and said, "If you were to write a sentence describing the glass of water you are holding, what would you say?"

I set the glass down and wrote, "The glass of water is half empty."

The adult looked at my sentence and said, "No, that is a negative sentence. You said the glass of water is half empty. Cross out the word *empty* and write the word *full*. That is a positive word."

I changed my sentence to say, "The glass of water is half full."

You must make every effort every day to be positive in your way of living, thinking, and feeling. When you do that, your English will be more positive. You can change the words around to make them more positive. This will help you develop the habit of being positive in whatever you do, even in difficult situations.

One sign I see many young people use which I don't like is the sign *can't. I can't, I can't, I can't* —I hate that sign. I hope all of you will throw the sign *can't* into your wastebasket. Throw it away and never pick it up again. Let your favorite sign be *can*. We deaf people can do anything if we are willing to try. Remember that.

An example of a person with a positive attitude is the famous man who invented the electric light bulb, Thomas Edison. How many times do you think he made mistakes before he succeeded in inventing the light bulb? I have asked many people around the country, and they have answered anywhere from a few to one thousand mistakes. Thomas Edison tried 17,143 times before he was successful in getting his light bulb to work. How many of you would be willing to make 17,143 mistakes before you succeeded once? I want you to remember when you make four or five mistakes in your English, you still have 17,139 more times to try before you succeed. But that is all right.

Mistakes can be wonderful teachers. Think of the pencil with an eraser on top. Why did the manufacturers make the pencil with an eraser? They make it because it is natural for people to make mistakes. It is all right, perfectly all right, to make mistakes. There is no shame in not knowing everything. Remember a pencil whenever you are in a situation and make a mistake.

Some years ago two famous deaf leaders, who didn't like each other, lived a block apart in a small town. Both of them were very successful in their areas of leadership, but they hated each other. When it came to leading and helping other people, though, they had a good "others before self" attitude. When the two of them were with a group, they understood that their personal feelings were secondary in importance. The cause they were helping with was of primary importance. They worked together, but they did not socialize at parties.

One afternoon the two men attended the same meeting. When they left the meeting and started home, it was raining hard. They lived near each other, and both decided to take the shortest and quickest way home. That way was via a railroad track, so they walked there together through the mud. One man had on a new pair of shoes, and he was worried that his shoes would get dirty. He suggested to the other man that they walk on the tracks, one man on each rail. It was hard to balance on one rail, but they tried it. It didn't work, so one man said to the other, "Why don't you walk on one rail, and I will walk on the other rail. Then if we reach out and clasp hands, our balance problem will probably be eliminated." It was and the two men arrived home without getting too muddy. They helped each other. That is an example of positive attitudes at work.

The last thing I would like to share with you in connection with attitude is that deaf youth around the country are afraid to ask questions. That is a mistake; it is almost a crime. When I was a little boy in the Minnesota School for the Deaf, I would not ask questions.

Why? I was stubborn for one thing. Also, I didn't want people to think I was dumb. I really didn't want my rival in school to know that I didn't know something. My rival and I competed for the best grades, for more points in games, and for girl friends. I often felt like a blockhead in school. The teacher would write many words that I didn't understand on the chalkboard, but I would not raise my hand and ask the teacher to explain. I knew that my rival would think I was dumb. But he raised his hand; he had a positive attitude. He had the courage to ask questions. "What does that word mean?" he would ask the teacher.

The teacher would write more sentences on the board to explain the word and its meaning. I didn't know the word, but I would look at my rival and say, "You don't know that word? That is a baby word. I learned it two or three years ago."

That was really a lie. He would get mad and sit there thinking about beating me up later instead of listening to the teacher. I was very calm, listening to the teacher and trying to learn. That was selfish of me, and I don't want you to be like that.

Many years ago I had in my office a newspaper clipping from New York City. It was a true story and it was very interesting. One day a boy was walking along a busy street in New York. He stopped and looked up at a nearby building—the Empire State Building. He stood there and kept looking up at the building. Other people walking along saw him looking up. They stopped and started looking up, too. Soon the people began talking to each other about why they were looking up at the building. Different stories got started. One story was that someone up there wanted to jump, to commit suicide. Another story was that a bomb was in the building. The police came and got all of the people out of the Empire State Building. They cleared it because they thought there was some kind of danger. Before long, all of the surrounding streets were full of cars and people. The area was paralyzed. Nothing could move. Police checked the building with dogs, but they found no bomb. Then they began asking around among the people to find out what the problem was. They finally found the boy standing there looking up, the one who started it all. The police learned that he was blind; he wasn't looking at anything, really. If the first person who saw the boy looking up had gone to the trouble of asking him what was wrong up there, all of these problems could have been avoided. Just asking a question was all that was needed.

Many words go by without your understanding them. Don't let that happen. Stop and ask someone what they mean. When they are explained, put them in your mental file cabinet. Don't be afraid to ask questions. Become the person you are meant to be.

Look or Listen

Ray S. Parks, Jr.

A long time ago, when I was sixteen, I got my driver's license. I wanted to drive, so I asked my dad if I could use his car. He thought about it and said, "Well, it will be okay, but only for short distances." I started driving his car for short distances. By the time I was seventeen years old, Dad saw that my driving was good, so he let me drive more. I felt so good in my dad's big Buick—at that time it was a great car—driving around waving at everybody. I enjoyed having people look at me.

One day I decided to drive up to the mountains. I saw a man hitchhiking. I pulled over, and he got in the car. He spoke to me, but I motioned to him that I couldn't hear. He looked at me and pointed for me to drive straight ahead. I nodded and drove on. As I was going up the road, I decided to pass a car. My passenger became nervous; he just couldn't sit still. He kept bothering me and saying, "You can't drive; you can't hear. How can you drive when you can't hear?" He kept saying the same things over and over.

Then I got an idea. I remembered that I had some tape in the glove compartment of the car. I pulled off to the side of the road. The man looked at me like he wanted to know what was going on. I motioned to him that he should drive. He thought that was a great idea. "Just a minute," I said. "You need to hear to drive, right?"

He said, "Yes, that's right."

So I tore off a piece of the tape, a big piece of tape, and put it over the man's eyes. Of course, he couldn't see. I said, "Okay, go ahead and drive."

"I can't drive," he said. "I can't see!"

He learned that you can drive without hearing but not without seeing.

The Case of the Missing Scissors

Barbara Kannapell

My father told me many stories. He was deaf and loved to tell stories in sign language. One story he told was about his father, my grandfather. One day my grandfather had to go to the hospital because he had trouble with his appendix. He had an operation and, a few days later, went home in a horse and buggy. When he arrived home, he still had pain in his side. The pain lasted for days, so grandfather had to go back to the hospital. The doctor said he would have to open the incision. When the doctor reopened the incision, he found a small pair of scissors inside my grandfather. After my grandfather learned this, he became furious and wanted to sue the hospital. His doctor was worried. He didn't want to be sued, so he said to my grandfather, "Okay, the operation and everything is free!"

That Look of Envy

Jack R. Gannon

My deaf friend Tom told me this story. I would like to share it with you. Tom had a beautiful car, a roadster (a sports car) called an MG. Tom was very proud of his car. It was a beautiful shade of red and it had shiny chrome.

One day after work, Tom was driving along on his way home. He stopped at a red light, and he noticed people glancing at him. He felt proud. The people were noticing his little red car. Feeling good, he shifted gears and revved up his car and drove on. Soon he arrived at another stop light. He noticed more people staring, more than before, and he felt inspired. He looked at his watch and drove on. When he arrived home, he drove into his driveway. His neighbor came running out, waving at him, and shouting, "Hey, Tom! Hey, Tom! Your horn is stuck!"

A Little Bit at a Time

Mary Beth Miller

I remember when I was a small girl, I loved to eat peanut butter. One day I told my mother I wanted a peanut butter sandwich. She said, "No, it is too close to dinner."

"Please," I said, but she replied, "No."

Again I said, "Please, I want a peanut butter sandwich."

My mother said no, again, and she looked angry.

I said, "Okay," and started to go outside. My mother had a visitor in another room, so she went in there.

As I was going out, I stopped, changed my mind, and went back into the kitchen. I opened the cupboard, took out a gigantic jar of peanut butter, unscrewed the lid, and took out a huge lump of peanut butter. Then I put the jar back. As I started out again, I saw my mother coming in. I was frightened because she had said that I couldn't have a peanut butter sandwich, but I had gotten some peanut butter to eat anyway. I quickly put the whole lump in my mouth. I swallowed, but the peanut butter got stuck. I started to choke on it; I couldn't breathe! I walked along the side of the house holding my throat. I felt faint and couldn't hold my head up.

The friend who was talking with my mother looked out the window and noticed that something was wrong with me. She said to my mother, "You had better check on your daughter; something may be wrong."

Mother opened the door and saw me there with my mouth open. She was scared. She thought something was stuck in my throat, but she didn't know what it was. She ran down the steps, took my legs, turned me upside down, and shook me up and down. People passing by stopped their cars and stared. They wondered what my mother was doing, shaking me up and down. Finally the lump of peanut butter came out. Then Mother turned me over and stood me up. She was surprised when she looked down and saw the lump of peanut butter. She thought maybe it had been a button or a coin that I choked on, but it wasn't. It was that peanut butter. Oh, my throat hurt! All my mother said was, "Well." But I learned my lesson. From that time on I've never taken a huge lump of peanut butter—only a little bit at a time.

5

The Importance of Bilingual Education for the Deaf

Barbara Kannapell

A few years ago I became interested in studying different sign languages and deaf people's use of different signs. Since I was studying sign languages, I decided to go to school and take some courses in sociolinguistics. I was fascinated to learn that foreign people's use of French and Spanish parallel deaf people's use of different sign languages. It was very interesting. Sociolinguistics itself tends to look at things in more positive ways.

More recently I investigated different professional textbooks about deaf children. I didn't realize that deaf people, including deaf children, are given so many negative labels. For example, some of the labels are language deficient; learning disabled, meaning one can't learn or has problems learning; and possessing a communication disorder. Do we have a communication disorder? No, we do not. We deaf adults and children do fine in sign language, but hearing people who evaluate us label us as language deficient. That is an error. I think the labels have influenced deaf children in how they feel about themselves. I think the labels have influenced how I feel about myself. I became negative, I had a negative self-image. I thought hearing people were better than I because they had fantastic English and good speech. Negative labels made me think this way.

Today, many people use total communication. Is that more positive? I think it is more positive to use different ways to communicate with deaf children. I notice many schools like the idea of using the term *total communication*. I notice many teachers speaking and signing at the same time, but that is all. I think total communication means using other methods, including ASL (American Sign Language). ASL is used by deaf people throughout the United States. If you include ASL, then I think that is the true meaning of total communication.

I want to suggest looking for more positive labels for deaf children. I also propose the idea of bilingual education for deaf children. They already know ASL, so why not help them make the connection between ASL and English. Really, deaf children know many things in ASL, but they don't know what those things mean in English. If the teacher knows English, but not ASL, and the deaf children know ASL, but not English, they can work together, exchange information, and help each other. For example, deaf children might say in ASL, "McDonald's is my favorite restaurant. It has delicious hamburgers." They can say this in signs, but they don't know how to write the English sentences. If the teacher knows ASL, she or he can explain how to write the words in English. That is why I like the idea of bilingual education for deaf children. If deaf children know both ASL and English, they can be called bilingual. Children who only know ASL can be called ASL monolingual, monolingual meaning one language. Deaf children who know only English can be called English monolingual. Deaf children need such positive labels to improve their self-image.

Life with Brian

Eric Malzkuhn

I am going to share some very wonderful moments of my life with you. I have three boys; no, really, I have four. The first three are my sons, and the fourth is my dog. My second son is deaf. (My dog is hearing, by the way.) I want to tell you about some incidents in the life of my deaf son which show the growth of his imagination and language, and his growth in other ways.

One early incident I remember happened one night while I was sitting very comfortably reading the newspaper. Brian, who was about three years old, ran up to me. He didn't have much language at that time. "Daddy, Daddy," he said.

"Yes, what is it?" I asked.

"Daddy, Daddy," he said again. Then he made a gesture which I had never seen before. It was very strange. I didn't know how to respond, so I got up and followed him. He ran quickly to the door; we opened it, and sure enough, I had forgotten something. It was Halloween. There stood a boy with a sheet on his head and a grimace on his face. Brian's gesture had very clearly communicated what it was. It was his own invention, and it was probably better than the sign "ghost."

As Brian grew a little older, he became interested in many things. Mostly he was interested in trains. He had many different kinds of trains, which I had given him, but I wanted to give him something related to his trains for Christmas. I tried to ask him what he wanted, but he didn't have the words to explain. I asked him what it looked like. He showed me, and it was obvious he wanted a semaphore for his trains. That was what I gave him for Christmas.

Our communication progressed. One day I had to go to the doctor. The whole family went with me. When we got to the office, we went in and sat down. Soon Brian became restless. He wanted to go over to the corner and play with the toys. I told him it was okay. A while later an old woman walked in and sat down in the chair Brian had used. Brian was busy playing; then suddenly he looked up and became very upset. He didn't like it that the woman was in his chair. Brian came over to the woman and said, "Hey." He tapped her on the leg and signed to her, "That's mine. That's mine. That's my chair." I didn't know what to do. I was so embarrassed; people were looking at me. I told Brian to be quiet. "That's wrong; it's mine; it's my chair," Brian said. The woman was quite uncomfortable so she got up and left. Later, I told Brian to be kind to ladies. That was one of his first lessons in life!

On one of my bowling nights I was backing out of the driveway when I saw Brian on his bicycle. He stopped, stood up on the seat, reached up, and pulled the fire alarm near our house. I stopped, ran inside, and told my wife that Brian had pulled the fire alarm. My wife said, "Really? That is your responsibility; you saw him." She was right, but I took off to bowl. My wife told me later what happened. Fire engines came racing up our street and stopped in front of our house. Brian was shocked, but fascinated. The fire chief strutted right up to our house and looked around. My wife wrote a note to the fire chief which said, "He did it." She pointed to Brian. My Brian was all starry-eyed. The fire chief looked down at him and asked, "You did it?" Then he began to speak rapidly.

My wife said, "Brian can't hear."

So the fire chief began to gesture. He said, "No, no, no. That is bad."

From then on when Brian went past a fire alarm, he said, "No, red box, no." Blue, red, and white box—a mail box—it was okay to pull down the handle, but not on a red fire alarm—no!

As Brian grew older, he began to understand more and more. His interests also began to change. One time he came home looking angry. "What's wrong? Why are you angry?" I asked him.

"I went to the boy's club," he said, "and the director told me to go home."

"What were you doing? Why were you sent home?" I wanted to know.

He answered, "I was playing."

"Playing," I said. "Brian, what were you playing?"

"I was playing the piano," he replied. I found out later why the director sent Brian home. (Remember, Brian is deaf, and he was playing the piano!) The director had gone to Brian and asked him what he was doing. Brian had responded, "I am playing the piano."

"No, you are not," the director said. "Go home."

Apparently Brian had hit the wrong chord or something.

This next incident demonstrates how Brian showed some interest in responsibility. He wanted to do things to help at home because he wanted an allowance. He asked me if he could do some work. I said he could and asked what he wanted to do? He didn't know. I suggested that he take his brother Max for a walk around the block. I told him I would pay him. That was fine with Brian, so he took his little brother, and they walked down the street. I watched them leave, and then I started working. A little while later Brian came back alone.

My wife looked at him and said, "Brian, where is Max?"

Brian said, "Poor Max, he was on the railroad tracks, and the train ran over him and he was cut in half. There was a lot of blood."

My wife got in the car and hurried to the train depot. She saw nothing; no one was there. Brian was sitting in the back seat of the car. "Where is Max," she asked again.

"Oh, he is in the cemetery," Brian answered.

My wife drove to the cemetery and there was Max, crying and crying.

Later my wife asked Brian, "Why did you tell that awful story?"

"Well," he said, "I wanted to make an interesting story." It was very interesting!

To show you that growth does not stop and older deaf people have problems occasionally, let me share a final experience I had with Brian. One day, while Brian was still living at home, my wife was obviously not feeling her best. How did I know? She began to slam the cupboard doors. (That is always my signal to sit down quietly and hide behind the newspaper. I peek out occasionally to see what is happening.) That day while I was hiding behind the newspaper, Brian walked into the house dribbling a basketball— pound, pound, pound—and went to his room.

In a little while I could see the walls vibrating. I went in Brian's room and found a big argument going on between him and his brother Max. "All right, settle down," I said. (I am a father so I have to play referee once in awhile.) I said to the boys, "What is the matter?" I heard one explanation and then the other explanation. Brian said Max was wrong, and Max said Brian was wrong.

It seems that Max had said to Brian, "Mother has a headache, and you are not helping any."

Brian had said, "I helped her all morning. I helped her clean the house."

You see, he misunderstood the idiom *not helping any*. To Brian it meant that he had not helped clean the house. To Max it meant that Brian's basketball dribbling bothered their mother; it was making things worse.

Brian is grown now, and he is a man in every sense of the word. He is a teacher of the deaf; maybe he faces the same problems that I faced. Although I think that Brian gave us a lot of problems and a lot of worries, if I had my way, I would have three more sons just like him!

6

Applause for Eyes to See

Bernard Bragg

I remember how excited I was when I sat down in front of the mirror, opened a jar of white clown make-up, and began to smear it on my face. Looking back, I remembered when I was a little boy, watching my father perform on stage, acting in sign language. I was both thrilled and motivated. I guess that was how I became interested in theater. Much later I met Marcel Marceau, the world-famous mime, and he invited me to Paris to study with him.

But there I was, sitting in front of the mirror in a dressing room of a nightclub. I picked up the black pencil and used it around my face, under my eyes, and around my lips. I put some red make-up on my lips. Then I began to feel a little nervous and scared because tonight I was going to do my first performance in that big place. A lot of people were coming to see me perform. Would I succeed, or would I fail?

Suddenly the door opened and the manager—Frey was his name—stuck his head through the door. "You're on," he said.

"Okay," I replied. I put on a red and white striped shirt and white pants and ran out on the dark stage. I stood and waited for the lights to go on. When they did, I saw many people sitting and looking at me. I performed several different sketches. People began to enjoy them, and they started to applaud after each one. I acted out different characters: An old lady hobbling along with a cane, a big pot-bellied man with a mustache and beard listening to his stopwatch, and a little boy hopping along with a dog on a leash. Finally I was done. I bowed and all the people clapped and cheered. Saying good-bye, I left the stage. After I left, the manager went on stage and stopped the applause. "It is no use to applaud," he told the people. "The man you just saw is deaf. So why applaud? Don't bother!"

I was in my dressing room. Someone came in and asked, "Do you know what Frey said?"

"No," I said, "what?"

"He said it is useless to applaud because you are deaf."

I was shocked. Because I'm deaf he was telling people not to applaud. I ran back on the stage. "Hold it, hold it," I told the audience. "I can't hear, it's true, but I have eyes and I can see your hands clapping. So come on, applaud." And, sure enough, all the people applauded. I said good-bye and left the stage again.

On My Own

Deborah M. Sonnenstrahl

When I was a little girl, about five years old, I went to an oral school in Baltimore, Maryland. At that time I was living in a house with my family which consisted of my mother and father, my grandmother and grandfather, and a great-aunt. Everyone had normal hearing except me. I was born deaf. Naturally, they made every effort to include me in all activities. They loved me, but sometimes I thought perhaps they loved me too much; I was overprotected. The result of that was that I often wanted to show my independence. I became rebellious from time to time. I wanted to show them I knew how to act like a grown-up. I was no exception; I was just like any other child.

One bright Saturday morning I made a formal announcement to my family. I said, "I am going out for a walk. I have decided where I will go."

My family said, "Oh, really! That's fine. Where are you going?"

"I am going to visit my school," I replied.

The oral school was about five blocks away from our house. Every morning the school bus came by, picked me up, and took me to school, but that special Saturday morning I wanted to walk to school. It didn't matter that the school was closed that day. That was not important to me. My grandmother opened the closet door and got her coat. She was ready to go with me. I asked her, "Where are you going?"

She answered, "I'm going with you."

"No," I said, "you are not going with me; I am going alone."

"Alone? No, no, no! You can't go alone."

"Why not?"

"But, Debbie, you live five blocks from school. You will have to cross busy streets. Cars will come, and they might hit you. You can't go alone; you can't hear the cars."

I had already made up my mind. "I am going alone!" I screamed.

Then my family started to argue among themselves. My mother and grandmother were saying, "No, no, she can't go, she can't go, she can't go." I started to cry. In the middle of all that my father stood up, thoughtfully surveyed the situation, and made up his mind. He said, "Let her go." He tapped me on the shoulder and said, "You can go alone."

"Oh, Daddy, Daddy!" I cried, jumping for joy. I put on my coat, scarf, and gloves. I was so excited! For the first time ever, I was going out in the world by myself. My mother cried. She looked at me; my grandmother looked at me; my great-aunt looked at me. My grandfather just stood by the door with his cane, acting very cool about the situation. My father, who was a pediatrician (a baby doctor), walked into his office. I waved good-bye to each member of the family. I kissed each one on the cheek and went out all by myself. I was alone, breathing in the fresh air.

It was a strange feeling. I was walking to school alone! On my way I began to notice things I had never seen before. I had passed this way many, many times with my mother, my grandmother, or my aunt. It didn't matter because they were always holding my hand and I was looking down. I never really looked at the world around me. But this time on my own, I started to look at things. I noticed my dentist's house. It had venetian blinds, and I had never seen them before. Oh, and a store had a special name printed on it! Another house had fancy flowers in front of it. I looked around and enjoyed my walk very much. I arrived at the first intersection and stood there. Oh, I felt so grown up; I felt so adult. I looked around for cars. When the coast was clear, I jumped across the street. I ran. I was safe. I was free! I felt so good.

I was walking the second block when I began to feel that something was strange, something was out of the ordinary. I looked around, thinking perhaps people were watching me. No, that wasn't it; people were passing by, and they were minding their own business. I looked up. There was nothing there. I felt strange, but I tried to ignore the feeling and continued walking.

In the third block the same thing happened. I felt strange again, so I hurried along. I reached the fourth block, and then I saw my school. Oh, this was my old friend where I spent five days a week. There it was, but I had the strange feeling again. Something was bothering me, but I saw nothing. Then I looked behind me. Do you know what? My father was following me! Oh, I felt defeated!

The Stand-in

Eric Malzkuhn

I am going to tell you about a precious moment in my life— something that will never happen to me again. While I was living in California, I taught several different kinds of classes. Two of the classes were drama classes. One was a class of slow learning students. For this class I picked a play called *Amahl and the*

Night Visitors, based on an opera by Gian Carlo Menotti. You have probably seen the play on television. The play was a good choice for the students in that particular class because the lines were not very long. The students struggled with the short lines. They memorized them. Then, they practiced and practiced and practiced. They worked hard for me. When opening night came and the curtain opened, I stood and watched. I just couldn't believe it. It was beautiful. The play was fantastic. The students did a fine job. I was so proud of the class because the play was a real success.

When the curtain closed, Johnny, who acted the part of Amahl, came up to me and said, "Hey, tomorrow I can't act in the play."

"What? You can't act?" I asked. "What are you talking about? What do you mean? People are coming tomorrow to see the play. You have to be here."

"Well," Johnny replied, "my father says I have to go to the dentist to have a tooth pulled."

Oh, no, I was stuck. What was I going to do? I thought and in a little while, I had an idea. Amahl was a crippled boy. Well, I am crippled, too; Amahl's leg was crippled like mine. Maybe I could change Amahl from the son to the father. I considered this and decided the change would be okay.

That night I went home and studied my lines. I studied them all night—all night, I tell you. But I wasn't alone. My three dogs helped me. Oh, they were wonderful. We paced back and forth, back and forth, all four of us. If I dropped a line, the dogs sat. If I messed up a line, the dogs barked. And if I just happened to be on the wrong page, my dogs growled. That way it was hard for me to make a mistake. I just followed what they told me to do while I practiced all night. The next day I drove to school. I felt tired, my eyes were blurry, and my mind was fuzzy, but I was excited. I was ready for the performance.

During the play I made one mistake, just one. The girl who played the role of the mother, you remember, was supposed to be a slow learner. I had changed the lead role from the son to the father. She had to call Amahl *father* instead of *son* all through the play. She didn't make a single mistake! Now who was slow and who was smart?

Our Paths Crossed Again

Thomas A. Mayes

I imagine that each of us, at one time in our lives, has had some experience, some encounter, which demonstrates that this world, even though it is 25,000 miles in circumference, with over 200 billion people, is really very small. I would like to share such an experience with you.

Back in 1960 I was a doctoral student at Michigan State University in East Lansing. One of the courses I took was a seminar called "Personnel Management in Higher Education." The group was small, about twelve people, but we had many interesting discussions. We decided that for the last meeting of the class we would invite the three highest administrators of the university — the president, the provost, and, of course, the football coach — to join us for dinner. We would talk with them and pick their brains.

It so happened that the man who sat next to me was the provost; his name was Paul A. Miller. Paul Miller, a very intelligent man, had a position of high authority in a university of forty to forty-five thousand students. I did not feel very comfortable sitting next to him, and I do not think he felt very comfortable sitting next to me. He had never seen nor met a deaf person before in his life, and I had never met a provost before. He had a feeling that if he talked to me, I would not understand him. And I felt, also, that if I talked to him, he wouldn't understand me. So Dr. Miller and I spent a very quiet evening together.

About a year later Paul Miller left MSU to become president of West Virginia University. He stayed there one or two years; then he became Assistant Secretary of the Department of Health, Education, and Welfare and moved to Washington, D.C. In that capacity, Dr. Miller served as a liaison to Gallaudet College, and he attended all of the Board of Trustee meetings on Kendall Green. He developed a very great interest in deaf people and in Gallaudet College. His relationship with Gallaudet grew stronger. About three years or so later, he moved to one of the southern states to teach, and then he went to the Rochester Institute of Technology in New York. There he was the president of the mother institution of the National Technical Institute for the Deaf.

Gallaudet College had faith in Paul Miller and wanted to continue its relationship with him. So the college invited Dr. Miller to serve on the Board of Trustees as a regular member.

Some years passed, and in 1968 I was invited to serve on the Board of Trustees. When I came to my first board meeting, I found myself sitting next to Paul A. Miller.

Caught in a Riot

Michael Schwartz

Once I was in Mexico with a group of high school students. We stopped in a town called Oaxaca. (It's a funny name, and I really don't know how to pronounce it.) We arrived there in a Volkswagen bus, maybe fifteen of us in all. When we got to Oaxaca, we spread out and went to different places. I was with one of my friends, and we decided to have something to drink. We went into a restaurant and ordered drinks. All of a sudden my friend heard some noise outside. He told me that he heard something, but he didn't know what it was. Then we saw some people running very quickly past the restaurant. Of course, we became curious. We wondered what they were doing, and where they were going. We decided to follow them.

We quickly paid the bill, went outside, and ran to catch up with the people. We began following them. When they turned a corner, so did we. We came to a stop across the street from a large building. People were throwing stones through the windows of the building. We learned that students inside the building had taken control of it. They had taken control of the building to publicize their demands. My friend and I—we were curious to find out more about what was going on—stayed there. That wasn't a smart thing to do because a few minutes later a big truck pulled up outside the building. A lot of men jumped out of the truck. It turned out that they were soldiers. Naturally, we were frightened, but we still stayed. We wanted to see what was going to happen. The students retreated inside the building and refused to come out. The soldiers became very angry and started shooting. My friend and I didn't know what to do, whether to stay or run. People were running about, and we had to make a decision. There was no more time to think.

We ran! We came to a church and went inside. Many other people were in the church because they thought they would be safe there. They knew that the soldiers wouldn't go in the church. While we waited, we remembered that we had come with a group, but now there was just the two of us. Where was the rest of the group? We didn't know. We were pretty scared because the soldiers were shooting and the people were throwing rocks. We stayed in the church and talked about what to do. Finally, we decided to leave and try to find the restaurant again. Maybe some people in our group would be there.

I thought I remembered the way, so we left the church and ran. I was right; we found the restaurant. Some of the people from our group were there. We all got together and ran back to the bus. By that time, the town was in an uproar. There was lots of noise— people running and shouting, soldiers shooting—it was really terrible. When we got in our VW bus, we took off like a shot. As we drove through the town, we saw some women carrying sticks. They were big, mean looking women. They were walking in the direction of the building where the students were. We didn't know why. Later we found out that the women were the mothers of the students, and they were angry with the soldiers for shooting at their children.

As I look back on that experience, I was afraid, nervous, and excited while it was happening. Now I'd like to have more experiences like that.

My ABC Book

Mary Beth Miller

For a long time I wanted to write a book, a sign language book. I thought about it, and finally I wrote an ABC book. Oh, it wasn't very good, but the drawings in it were fine. My problem was how to get it published.

One day I flew to Paris, France, and met my friend Remy. I told him that I wanted to publish my ABC book. He asked to see it, so I showed him the book. He thumbed through it and then put it down. He said he too wanted to publish a book, an ABC book. He asked if we could work together on one. I agreed. I was so excited when I returned to the United States.

Several months passed, and then Remy and I met again. We had to make plans for our book. What words and pictures would we use for the letters of the alphabet? What would stand for the letter *A*? *Angel*. What would we use for the letter *B*? *Bug, butterfly*. We had to make decisions about words and signs for all the letters. Then I called some friends and asked them if they wanted to have their pictures taken for the book Remy and I were writing. They accepted gladly, so we had many pictures taken.

The photographer, George, couldn't sign; he didn't know signs at all. If I talked to him, he didn't understand, so we struggled, writing notes back and forth. Remy knew signs a little bit. He wasn't skilled in signing, but he tried hard to communicate. The three of us managed to work well together on the book. When George finished taking all the pictures, we met to choose the ones to use. We looked through thousands of pictures, throwing out the lousy ones and keeping the good ones. While we worked, my two friends improved their signing. George, who couldn't sign at first, learned *thank you, happy, play, picture, now, again,* and many other signs. Remy, who could sign some, improved and became a very good signer.

When the book was published and I received a copy, I was very proud. I felt good. Seeing it gave me goose pimples. I was extremely happy. Remy and George were happy, too. Our book was finished, and it was beautiful. I was happy because many of my friends' pictures were in the book. Now every day I can look at our book and think about my many wonderful friends!

7

Deaf Pilots

Jack R. Gannon

I have learned, to my surprise, that through the years many deaf people have been licensed to fly planes. Almost one hundred deaf people have probably received a license at one time or another.

Nellie Willhite of South Dakota was the first woman and the first deaf person in the United States to get a pilot's license. She was a very successful pilot. She barnstormed around the Midwest, going to county fairs and doing stunt flying for crowds of impressed people. When she landed, she offered rides to the people, charging fifty cents for children and a dollar for adults. The first deaf man in this country to get his license to fly was John Stirling. This was in 1937. Ten years later, Rhulin Thomas, another deaf man, flew a small Piper Cub from Delaware to the west coast, becoming the first deaf person to fly solo across the United States.

I called the FAA, the Federal Aviation Agency, and inquired as to how many licensed pilots today are deaf. I was told that about twenty-five pilots are deaf. One of these is a commercial pilot. How about that?

Experience Is a Great Teacher

Florence B. Crammatte

E xperience is a great teacher. It teaches us many things: happiness and sadness; excitement and tranquility; success and failure; and from all these we learn wisdom. We learn a lot of information from books, but what we learn from experience makes a deeper impression on us and stays in our minds much longer.

In our lives we have many experiences that are ordinary and pass from our minds quickly. Other experiences have a profound impact on our lives. I have two experiences from my youth I would like to share with you.

While I was in school at the Alabama Institute for the Deaf, there was a very fat little girl there who was about ten years old. Her name was Annie, and she had a strange body odor. No matter what was done—washing two or three times a day, or changing her clothes every day—she still had this strange odor. Children can be cruel to each other; they criticized and insulted Annie constantly. The other children held their noses or ran the other way when they saw Annie coming. I was guilty of doing that. When I went home for the summer, I described Annie to my mother with much disgust. My mother looked sad and said, "Poor child." That was all she said. I was somewhat nonplussed. Through the summer I often remembered what my mother had said, and my attitude became more understanding. I began to understand how Annie must have felt, and I resolved to be nice to her.

That fall Annie did not come back to school, and I never saw or heard of her again. That lesson has stayed with me through all these years. I have tried to be understanding of people who have faults or problems they cannot help. I try to help people who are shy, or who have bad tempers, or have a hard time explaining their ideas; newcomers who feel uncomfortable; or people who might lack self-confidence.

The other experience, one which I cherish, happened during my first year at Gallaudet College. I was seventeen years old then. We had a very active chapter in the YWCA (Young Women's Christian Association). The most enthusiastic supporter was Dr. Elizabeth Peet, the Dean of Women. For our Christmas project we decided to buy twelve dolls, sew clothes for them, and give them to poor children. One night the chapter president brought in twelve dolls and gave them out. Dr. Peet was with us that night, and she suggested that we give a tea when we had finished dressing the dolls. We would invite the students and faculty to see our efforts. Dr. Peet would give prizes for the prettiest doll, the neatest doll, and the most colorful doll.

My friend Isobol* and I worked together on a doll. Another girl, Ruth, quickly went to her closet, pulled out one of her most beautiful evening gowns, and began to rip it up to make a dress for her doll. When Isobol and I saw that, we decided we couldn't compete with her for the most beautiful doll, so we decided to try for the neatest doll.

We worked hard on our doll and her clothes. We sewed with care and patience. On the day of the tea we placed our doll among the other dolls. They had been placed on a long table in the girls' reading room. What a lovely sight they were! There was Ruth's doll in a beautiful blue taffeta dress with ruffles down the skirt, and little pink flowers all over. Our doll was dressed in a white blouse, plaid skirt, and plaid beret. Dr. Peet was one of the judges and she announced the winners. Ruth's doll won the prize for having the prettiest dress. Dr. Peet said the judges had trouble deciding which was the neatest doll. They felt that our doll should win, but there was something not quite right about it. She picked up our doll and pointed to some threads, little threads hanging from one sleeve and from the skirt. She said they should have been cut off. How crestfallen we were! The prizes were one dollar each. That was in the days of the Great Depression, and one dollar was a good amount of money.

Isobol and I learned our lesson, and I have never forgotten it. Everytime I sew, I think about Dr. Peet and that doll. When I finish sewing something, I look it over inside and out to make sure no threads are hanging.

---

*My friend Isobol later married an Episcopal minister. He was a minister to the deaf in northern New York State.

I cherish that small memory of Dr. Peet and me. I have told the story many times. I told it to my two daughters when they started sewing. Both of them had a good laugh, but I know that they remember the story and they have learned from it, too.

U.S.S. *Thomas Hopkins Gallaudet*

Jack R. Gannon

D id you know that during World War II there was a ship named after Thomas Hopkins Gallaudet? The ship was christened with a bottle of champagne by Pearl S. Buck, the famous author. I don't remember the exact words she used, but she said something like this, "This ship was built by strong hands and named after a wonderful soul. Let this ship sail across the rough seas just like Gallaudet himself did."

After the ship was christened, it was loaned to Russia under the United States' lend-lease program. Russia used it during World War II. When the war was over, the Russians gave the ship back to America. For several years it was sold and resold; it was used by different countries for a variety of things.

Sometime in 1969, the ship was sailing from Guam to South Korea with a full load of scrap iron. It was hit by a bad storm and broke into two pieces. It sank off the coast of Japan. It was really sad, but the ship had served all over the world for thirty-five years.

Here We Go Again

Nancy Rarus

I am from a deaf family. My parents, my grandmother and grandfather, and my brother are all deaf. When I was growing up, I signed all the time. Oh, my mother and father required me to talk, too. My father always spoke to me in straight English. My mother did too. I went to a public school (P.S. 47) all through my childhood. The teachers there slapped my hands and wouldn't allow me to sign. At home I could sign, so I was safe.

When we sat around the dinner table at home, my mother would always say to my father, "Stop talking and let the children eat before the food gets cold." My father would answer, "No, the food is still hot." Then they would argue about that. The point is that when we were growing up, my mother and father always shared information, world news, and gossip with us. I enjoyed that.

I remember when I was at school, I would bring home a girl friend. The best part of her visit was the communication at the dinner table, the family discussions. We sat at the table a long time. My mother, who is a perfect housekeeper, liked to clean up as soon as possible. Most evenings she had to sit and wait for us to finish our discussions.

When I was in college and brought home a friend, we went through the same thing. One friend of mine had a huge family, she had many brothers and sisters. Her family always just sat and ate. Then they excused themselves and left the table. At my home it was different. This is one good memory I have of growing up in a deaf family.

I often went to visit deaf girl friends at their homes. Their parents were hearing. They couldn't communicate, so they wrote notes. I thought, "Hearing parents are writing notes with their children?" Oh, I felt bad for them. I realized how lucky I was.

My father was a very good speech teacher. He taught me many ways to pronounce different words; he even taught me some French words. He would correct me when I made mistakes. Now I don't have problems with the words he taught me, even the big words. I may have problems with small easy words—sometimes I can't say them to save my life—but big words like *gesundheit* I am skilled at; I can say those!

I remember something else from when I was small. I got so tired of my parents' friends who came to visit and said, "Oh, I remember when you were small; you were so cute. Now you are big. You have really grown." I would say, "Yeah." Sometimes they would say, "I doubt if you remember me. You were small. . . ."

It was the same old thing. I said to myself, "In the future, when I grow up, I will not say those things to children." But I have to admit that I have been doing exactly the same thing. I guess it is part of human nature that we say those things.

Another thing that bothers me is how fast rumors spread among deaf people. Children of hearing parents are really lucky. Often the parents know nothing of what is happening with their deaf children. If I did something I didn't want my parents to know, I did it and that was it. However, soon there would be a tap on my shoulder. My parents knew; the rumors had spread like wildfire. I sympathize with deaf children with deaf parents because I know what they're going through.

Now, the tables are turned. I have two deaf children. I remember when my first child was born, the doctor informed me that he was deaf. I looked at the doctor and said, "He's deaf! Ah, here we go again."

The Letter I Wrote, but Never Mailed

Barbara Kannapell

I was born deaf to deaf parents. It seems that it would have been easy for them to make a decision about which school was best for me, but that was not true. I think it was difficult because of the pressure of hearing relatives. For example, my grandmother worried about me. She wanted me to have good training in speech and lipreading. My parents sent me to a public school which had a special class for deaf children. I was four, and I remember that time very clearly. I went into the school and I tried to learn to talk and lipread, but when I went home, I signed to my parents.

One day a well-known person, Mrs. Spencer Tracy, came to visit the school. (She is famous for promoting the oral method and for teaching parents how to communicate with young deaf children.) Mrs. Tracy stood next to my grandmother, both of them watched me. Mrs. Tracy looked down at me—she looked so tall to me—and said, "How are you?"

I replied, "I am fine." I spoke; I didn't sign.

She said, "Oh, that is wonderful; that is marvelous."

That's all I can remember that happened to me in the oral school where I remained for six years. Then I transferred to a school for the deaf. I don't know why or how, but all of a sudden I transferred to the Kentucky School for the Deaf.

I entered my first class in that school in the middle of the school year. My mother and I went into the classroom, and the woman who would be my teacher came up to me. She said, "Take your coat off."

I didn't understand her so I looked at my mother for help. My mother remained quiet, so I looked back and the teacher said, "Take your coat off."

I still didn't understand her so I looked at my mother again. She was still quiet; I looked back at the teacher. I struggled for several minutes. Finally I understood—she wanted me to take my coat off. I took it off and hung it up.

That school emphasized oralism even though the teachers used signs. The good thing about the school was that I could use signs with deaf children outside and then use the oral method in the classroom. When I transferred to a third school, it was even better because the teachers used signs, and the children used signs. Only the supervisors did not use signs; they couldn't sign! Can you imagine that the supervisors, who took care of the children every night after school, looked after them, and supervised them, didn't know how to sign? When I did something wrong, the supervisor would slap my hands, but she couldn't sign at all. Sometimes I wanted to tell her what was wrong—that she should let me explain and that she shouldn't slap my hand—but the supervisor would say no and shake her head. That was it. I never thought of a supervisor as my friend.

Recently I found my old suitcase and opened it. Instantly I spotted a letter. "What's that?" I thought. I didn't remember writing a letter. The envelope was addressed to the superintendent of the school I attended. I was curious as to what I had said in the letter. I opened it and was surprised to read the things I wrote. It said something like this: If I had my way, I would make all supervisors learn sign language. It's too bad I never sent the letter to the superintendent of the school. Today, I notice many teachers learning signs and more supervisors learning them, too. I think that is marvelous!

My Present Aspiration

Ray S. Parks, Jr.

I would like to tell you how it feels growing up as a deaf person, and how I feel as a deaf person today. I can remember where I went to school when I was five years old, and what it was like growing up in a school for the deaf. I would go away to school in the fall and come home in the summer. I attended that school from the time I was five until I graduated from high school. I loved the school; many things were good in that school, but still, there were a few things that I didn't like that could have been changed.

I attended Gallaudet College and I enjoyed my years there. I became a teacher, and after college I taught in several different schools for the deaf. I found a lot of things in these schools that I really didn't like, things that I thought could be better. However, the administration acted like it was frozen; it was like the administrators were afraid to change things. They felt that if they changed, everything would be chaotic. Things had to be kept under control, and all the children had to fit into one mold.

I saw this happening, and I didn't like it. I wanted the children to develop independent thinking, to think freely, but it never happened. As a result I decided to get out of the educational world and join the National Theatre of the Deaf (NTD). During my two years with them as an actor, I thought I was out of the educational world and in the world of the theater. I was wrong; while I was with NTD, I became more and more immersed in the educational world. I traveled to schools, gave workshops, and developed plays and similar things for the schools. I found that I was even more sensitive to the situations in the schools; the things I had seen as a teacher.

After two years with NTD I decided to go to New York University and study for a Ph.D. in Educational Administration. I wanted to become a school administrator. At NYU I learned a lot of things about administration, and I began to understand why some of my previous administrators had done certain things. I remembered the children complaining to me, but their words had never gotten through the superintendent's door. When I became an administrator I want to keep the door open.

Now I am traveling back and forth between New York and Philadelphia to do my administrative internship at the Pennsylvania School for the Deaf. My intern program is under the headmaster of the school. He has taught me many things about administrative policies, and I have become much more sensitive to the responsibilities of people in that area. I hope after I get my Ph.D. that I am going to become an administrator. When I do, I want to make things a lot better for the children in the school where I work.

8

Lessons Learned from My Elders

Frank R. Turk

As the director of Junior National Association of the Deaf (Jr. NAD), I naturally love young people, and I like to talk to them. Many young people have asked me this question, "When you were in school, from whom did you learn the most?" I have answered them, "Deaf adults." Young people are puzzled with this answer. They tell me they mean whom did I learn the most from when I was in school. Again I say, "Deaf adults taught me the most." They have looked at me and said, "You misunderstood us. We are talking about when you were small and in school." Then, they ask me which school I was in. I reply, "I attended the Minnesota School for the Deaf, MSD." "From whom did you learn the most at MSD?" they ask. Again, my answer is deaf adults. It's true that I learned more from deaf adults than from books, classroom lessons, or anything else. I will give you some examples of what deaf adults themselves taught me while I was growing up, things I still remember to this day.

One deaf adult, an old man, complained about the way I dressed. He noticed that I dressed the same way every day. Whether it was Monday, Tuesday, Wednesday, Thursday, or Friday, I always wore a white shirt and a tie. The old man didn't like that; he wanted to help me improve my appearance. He asked me, "Frank, why don't you have variety in your clothes?" I didn't understand what he meant.

"It's fine to wear a white shirt and tie on Monday," he said. "But Tuesday, why don't you wear something different? You could wear a bow tie and maybe a beige shirt. Then Wednesday, change to a different tie with a yellow shirt. Thursday, perhaps you could wear a blue shirt and maybe a bow tie again. Friday, it would be okay to go back to a white shirt and tie, or bow tie, or whatever you choose. Try wearing different clothes each day. Impress people with your variety of taste in clothes."

That adult taught me many things about clothes and appearance. I took his advice because I respected him.

About two weeks later I bought a bow tie. Then I went to my room and tried to tie it. I tied it, but it didn't come out right. I took it off and tried to tie it again. It was hard, but I kept trying. Finally, I gave up. I went back to town and bought a bow tie with clips which fasten on the shirt collar. It was easier to put on because I didn't have to tie it. That kind of tie is for lazy people! I put it on and looked in the mirror. The tie looked nice. But I forgot one important thing. While clip ties are easy to put on, they also fall off easily. Whenever I signed to my teachers or friends, my tie began to fall off. I would clip it back on, but it would start to fall off again. This happened several times before I took the bow tie off and went back to a four-in-hand tie. Change to a bow tie? Forget it!

A few months later the old deaf man came back to school and looked me up. I was still Frank, but there was some improvement. I was wearing a beige shirt.

"Oh, I see you have a beige shirt," the man said to me. "Well, that is fine. What about the tie?"

I explained that I tried bow ties. One I couldn't tie, and the other one fell off.

He looked at me and asked, "How do you tie your shoe laces?"

I was disgusted that he would ask me a baby question like that. I knew how to tie my shoe laces.

He continued, "Do you know that you tie a bow tie the same way you tie your shoe laces?"

I didn't know that. I went to my room and stood in front of the mirror. I tied the bow tie like I tied my shoe laces. That was it. It worked! The old man taught me something that no one in school ever had time to teach me.

Another deaf adult taught me something important about hunting. He asked me, "When you are hunting on a windy day, do you hunt against the wind or with the wind?"

I explained that if it was a cold day and I faced the wind, my nose would freeze, so I would turn around. I hunted with the wind.

He said, "You never killed a deer, right?"

I replied, "That is right, but I try to improve."

"You are never going to improve," he said, "unless you suffer some." He explained that when you hunt with the wind, it is easy and comfortable for you, but you never see a deer. However, many deer see you and run away and hide. This happens because the wind carries your odor to the deer. When deer smell a human body, they run and the hunter doesn't see them.

I learned from that deaf adult that if I wanted to be a successful hunter, I had to hunt against the wind. If the deer don't know I am there, the chances are better that I will get a deer.

Another adult I remember very well asked me a question when I was about ten years old. He asked me to name the five Great Lakes. It is hard when you are young to remember their names. I told him that Lake Michigan was one. Then there was Lake Erie. But I wasted time trying to think of the other names. The adult asked me to spell the word *homes*. "H-o-m-e-s," I said.

"All right," he continued, "you can remember the five Great Lakes by putting the word *homes* in your mental file cabinet."

Now if you ask me the names of the five Great Lakes, I take the word *homes* out of my mental file cabinet and tell you, "*H*, Huron; *O*, Ontario; *M*, Michigan; *E*, Erie; *S*, Superior." That is an easy way to remember them. I learned many mental crutches from that adult. A mental crutch is a word you use to help you remember something. It is like using a crutch to help you walk when you break your leg.

I learned other mental crutch words from that adult. For example, the word *faces* helps me remember the five requirements for a person to be physically fit. The five requirements are: *F* - flexibility; *A* - agility; *C* - coordination; *E* - endurance; and *S* - strength. FACES! Oh, I have many memory crutch words in my mental file. If people ask me something, I use my crutch, and they think I'm smart. Really, I am clever. You don't have to be smart to do things like that. You just have to have the ideas; look for clever ways to remember things. I learned that from adults.

An interesting thing I learned from another adult was about accidents. One day the adult asked me, "If a person hit his head and was bleeding excessively, what would you do?"

I was small, and I looked at him and said, "I'd take off my shirt and wrap it around his head."

"Well, then what would you do?" he asked.

I said that I would telephone for an ambulance.

"No, you can't," he replied, "there are no hearing people here to make the call. So, what would you do?"

"My friend over there has a car," I said.

"Well, that is good," the adult said. "You put the man in the car to drive him to the hospital. Where is the hospital?"

"Oh, I know where it is. It is over there about four or five miles."

"Is that the road that leads to the hospital?" he asked me.

I told him that it was.

"What is the speed limit?" he wanted to know.

"It is 50 or 60 miles an hour, I guess," was my reply.

"Oh, no," he said. "It is 25 miles an hour. That is the speed limit. But do you have to drive that speed?"

I said, "No, I would go 50 or 60 miles an hour to save a life."

"You are right," he replied. "Now suppose a police car came up behind you with its siren on. What would you do?"

"I would show the police the injured man."

"No, you can't move or lift him," he continued. "You have to keep the man quiet. It is dangerous to move him."

"Well, I would pull over and stop," I said.

"You don't have time because the man is bleeding," the adult told me. "You have to hurry to the hospital. He may be dying."

I said, "Maybe I could write a note to the police."

"If you try to write and drive at the same time, you could go in the ditch," he said.

"Oh, that is right. What do I do?"

My adult friend said, "It is easy. Roll down the window as you are driving. Wave anything white, like a handkerchief, at the police officer. The officer will understand that *white* means you want to go to the hospital. The police officer will pull in front of you and lead you to the hospital with the siren on."

I remembered that several years ago when one of my children got hurt. A pot of coffee spilled on his back. The pain was terrible. I put him in the car and started driving to the hospital. My son was screaming and crying. A police officer came along, so I rolled down the window and waved a white handkerchief. It worked; the police officer led me by the shortest route to the hospital. An adult taught me that, and it helped my son and me.

One adult I owe a lot to is Chester C. Dobson, my favorite teacher in school. When I was in school, I wanted most of all to have good English language skills. You know that almost all deaf people want good language. If you have that, your friends will think you are a smart person. I knew people would respect me if I used good English. I wondered why it was so hard for me to master English. Why, for example, did I write and throw away piles of papers, but succeed in writing only one short sentence of four or five words? I felt dumb. I was afraid I was a hopeless case. My friends saw me writing and throwing papers out, maybe the three hundredth draft of something. I didn't want them to think I was dumb.

I asked Mr. Dobson, my favorite teacher, why my language was so weak. His answer was, "Frank, you have too much pride. You are not willing to make mistakes in exchange for improvement."

I looked at him and said, "That's right, I really have a lot of pride, but I want to improve now."

He told me that I never took on leadership responsibilities in a club, the student body government, Junior NAD, or any similar group. I looked at him strangely; I didn't see any connection between holding office and acquiring good English. Then he explained that taking a leadership role would help improve my English. After he said that, I understood, so I decided to run for an office. I had to improve my language before I graduated. I had to be able to write, read, and understand well.

I asked my friend Marilyn to nominate me for president of the drama club. I wasn't skilled at drama, but I wanted to get the benefit of improving my language from leading a group, as Mr. Dobson had explained to me. My girl friend said, "Okay, Saturday I will nominate you."

That was on Monday. Monday night I couldn't sleep; I tossed and turned. I was worried about my rival. In school all boys and girls have rivals competing for offices, like president of a club, for the best grades, for captain of the football or basketball team, or for getting the most points. How I disliked my rival. If I stood up as president and made a mistake, he would laugh and say, "Ha, you dumb cluck." No, I wasn't going to give him that opportunity. So I decided not to run for office.

Tuesday morning I met Marilyn and said, "Don't bring up my name Saturday. Drop it." But during the day my conscience bothered me. Mr. Dobson was right. I should be willing to make mistakes in exchange for learning. I met Marilyn again and said I still wanted her to nominate me on Saturday. Tuesday night I had another sleepless night, tossing and turning because of my rival. The next morning I told Marilyn again to drop it. Every day that week I changed my mind. I would tell her to nominate me; then I would tell her not to do it. Finally I decided to let her nominate me.

At the meeting my name was put on the chalkboard: Frank Turk. I looked at it and I was scared! I was hoping a lot of other students would be nominated, too. If I lost, I could always tell Mr. Dobson that I tried. That would be better than chickening out. But no one else was nominated, and I was elected president by acclamation.

Many names were listed on the board to be vice-president. There was a lot of arguing and excitement about that position, but I didn't pay any attention. I was busy thinking of what I would say to the club. They always asked the new president to make a few remarks or explain how he or she planned to improve things in the club. I had to think up some sentences to say. When the secretary and treasurer were elected, they called me, the new president, to go forward and say a few words. I wasn't scared when I got up because I had the words and sentences in my head. I walked to the stage, started up the steps, and fell! All the words I had thought of fell out of my mind; they disappeared! I stood up and left.

The next year I volunteered for a different office, but the same thing happened. I sat there, wrestling with words to say. Talking in front of people still bothered me, but I didn't want it to bother me. I started walking up the steps and fell again. Most of the words left me, but I kept one or two that time, so I had a few to start with. I was improving a little bit. The following year I volunteered for another office. I saw the faces of the people around me, and then I realized that we were all the same. I knew I had improved during the past year. Now if I fell, everything would stay in my mind. It wouldn't make any difference; it was like the words were taped in my mind.

Mr. Dobson taught me that leadership can be your best twenty-four-hour a day teacher. I understood that to lead a group successfully you must first be a clear thinker. Clear thinking requires good language, and good language requires planning and practice. For example, if I have to speak somewhere now, I plan the speech and practice it the night before. I go over what I am going to say again and again. The next day I can give the speech smoothly. That was what Mr. Dobson meant. By volunteering to take active roles in organizations, you have opportunities to develop better language. That can be your best English teacher.

Bar Talk

Jack R. Gannon

D o you know who B.B.B. is? B.B.B. is Byron B. Burns. He was the president of the National Association of the Deaf for many years—eighteen years in a row, I think. Let me tell you a short funny story about him.

One day B.B.B. decides to stop by a local bar after work to have a drink. He was tired and wanted to sit down and rest a bit. He entered the bar, walked up to the counter, and sat down. Noticing a man next to him, B.B.B. took out his pencil and pad and started to write. He introduced himself to the man, and they began a nice conversation. After awhile another hearing man came in and sat down next to B.B.B. B.B.B. felt this man should be included also, so he wrote back and forth between the two men. B.B.B. was deaf and the other two men were hearing, but they got along just fine. The three of them had a good conversation with pad and pencil.

Later B.B.B. looked at his watch. Wow! It was getting late! It was best for him to go home; his wife was waiting for him. He wrote,

"Excuse me, I have to go now. I enjoyed talking with both of you. Good-bye."

As he was going out the door, B.B.B. looked back. He saw that the two hearing men were still writing notes back and forth to each other. B.B.B. shrugged his shoulders and left.

9

Through an Act of God

Deborah M. Sonnenstrahl

I want to share a true story with you. It is about a famous sculptor who lived in the nineteenth century, quite a while ago. His name was Daniel Chester French. He did two famous statues. One is the Gallaudet Group. It is a statue of Thomas H. Gallaudet, father of Dr. Edward Gallaudet, who was the first president of Gallaudet College. The statue shows Thomas Gallaudet sitting and holding a deaf girl, his first student. He is teaching her the first letter of the alphabet. His arm is around the girl and she is looking up at him, making the letter "A." It is a very impressive statue. The other statue Mr. French did was the Abraham Lincoln Memorial in Washington, D.C. It shows Lincoln sitting with his arms on the arms of a chair. It is very popular in Washington; many tourists visit the Memorial every year.

But let's go back to the Gallaudet statue. When Dr. Gallaudet was president of Gallaudet College, he and the alumni group asked Mr. French, the sculptor, to sculpt the statue of Thomas Gallaudet. Mr. French thought it over. He had never had any association with deafness. He had heard a lot about the wonderful things Gallaudet College was doing with deaf people. So he visited Gallaudet College and looked over the beautiful campus and its buildings. He walked all around. Then he said, "I think I will accept the job. I accept the commission." Everyone was excited and very happy because Mr. French was already a well-known sculptor.

People asked the sculptor where he was going to put the statue. Mr. French said, "I will have to walk around the campus once more just to make sure that I pick the right location for the statue."

One beautiful day he walked all over the campus—the front, the back, and even in the fields. He walked along Florida Avenue, the street in front of Gallaudet College. He looked and made notes. He looked some more and made several sketches. Then he went to Dr. Gallaudet and told him, "I have the perfect place for the Gallaudet statue."

"Really?"

"Yes!"

"Where?"

Mr French said, "Exactly in front of the college itself, facing the college with the back to Florida Avenue where people passing by can glance at it."

The alumni thought it was the perfect place, right in the center of everything. However, a few people on campus were unhappy. The unhappy people were Dr. Gallaudet's children. You must remember that in the past, and even today, some of the college's presidents have lived on campus in a big house. Dr. Gallaudet and his family lived on campus. His children played on campus and also played with the students. Everyone knew each other very well.

The children were unhappy about the place chosen for the statue because that location had a large and beautiful tree, an oak tree, I think. Its trunk and limbs were thick. The tree was very old; it had seen many, many days. The children had a swing in the tree. This place was their favorite playground. But Mr. French, that mean old man, wanted to put the statue right in the middle of their play area. That meant someone would have to cut the tree down. That was unheard of! What a terrible thing! That tree was their beloved playmate. It protected the children from rain, and on warm days they sat beneath it in its cool shade. The sculptor was going to kill a friend! The children ran home. They argued with their parents. They told Dr. Gallaudet, "You can't do that to us; you can't, you can't, you can't!"

Dr. Gallaudet, like all good fathers, didn't want to hurt his children. As president of Gallaudet College, he had to think of some way to solve the problem. He was torn between the alumni group and his children. So he told the alumni group, the children, and Mr. French, "Let me think it over. Let me sleep on it." That poor man! He had a burden on his shoulders. He went home and got ready for bed.

During the night there was a terrible storm—lightning, thunder, and rain. It rained all night. In the middle of the night the family heard something—a very loud thump! Dr. Gallaudet looked out the window, and do you know what? The tree was hit by lightning!

The result was that Mr. French was happy. The alumni group was happy. Were the children happy? No, no, no! But through an act of God, Mr. French got his wish.

Sink or Swim

Michael Schwartz

W hen I was a small boy in Chicago living with my family, every weekend we'd go to the swimming pool at a high school in that city. There was a swimming instructor at the pool. I wasn't permitted to go into the deep end of the swimming pool—never in the deep end because all the big boys played there. I was only allowed to say in the shallow end where the little children stayed.

One day, I remember it very well, my parents were watching me, a group of other children, and the teacher. I was so excited that I swam with my head under water without really looking to see where I was going. I continued to swim and it was great! I swam and swam, and when I stopped, I found myself in the deep end of the pool.

At that moment I looked up and saw my mother. She was panicked. I had to think fast. I was in the deep end of the pool where everyone had told me I couldn't swim. I was taking lessons in the shallow end so that I could learn how to swim, but here I was in the deep end of the pool. I took a deep breath and swam all the way back to the other end of the pool. I got there safely, and my mother was so relieved. I thought to myself that everyone had told me I couldn't swim there, but when the moment came and I had to swim, I did.

Now I'm a student at New York University School of Law. I remember that before going to NYU, I said to myself, "I can't do it. It will be too much work for me." Then I thought of my earlier experience. I pictured swimming to the deep end of the pool, being stuck, and swimming back. I did it! Here I am in school and doing well. I just *thought* that I couldn't do the work at NYU. What is the moral of the story? You can do whatever you need to do. It really is possible!

How I Lied My Way to the Bottom

Thomas A. Mayes

D eaf people always have a very difficult time finding work in professional fields. As I look back at my younger days when I was first out of college, I recall such experiences. I think sometimes that time stands still.

When I graduated from the University of Chicago, I started out to look for work. My goal was to become an advertising copywriter. I quickly learned some hard facts of business life, including the fact that advertising people did not have an open heart for deaf individuals. The largest national advertising agencies in Chicago were located in tall buildings on North Michigan Boulevard, so I went to the Palmolive Building and took an elevator up to the top floor. I started with an agency called Batten, Barton, Durstein and Osborne. That company was and is very famous because when we say that name it sounds like a trunk falling down the stairs.

I went to the office of the Personnel Manager. He looked at me, the first deaf person he ever met, and said to himself, "My Lord, what a lot of nerve!" Then he got himself together and said, "Young man, how much experience have you had?"

I replied, "None really. I just graduated from college, but I am young, full of energy and ready to work."

"I'm afraid we can't take you," he said. "In this business we always look for experienced people. I'm sorry. Try something else."

So I moved down floor by floor and got the same reaction from other agencies. By the time I came to the fourth floor, I decided to lie a little bit. I said, "Well, I had two years experience working in small businesses writing advertisements." It didn't work, so I lied a little bit more about my experience—four years, five years, and so on. By the time I hit the ground floor, I was really the most polished liar ever to graduate from the University of Chicago.

What I Learned about Irish Sign Language

Bernard Bragg

What I enjoyed most about my world tour a few years ago was learning foreign sign languages. They all look different. I learned Russian, Finnish, Swedish, Norwegian, Irish, and Spanish sign languages—I visited twenty-five different countries. I found I was able to learn sign language very quickly. Also, I found that I was able to completely erase the one I had just learned from my mind just as quickly so I could learn another foreign sign language when I moved on.

I remember when I arrived in Dublin, Ireland, I met a very nice young couple, a married couple, who offered to show me around town. That was fine. We spent the whole day visiting the big, beautiful town of Dublin. The husband drove the car, and the wife sat next to him so she could point out the different sights to me. I sat in the back seat. As she described the sights to me, I learned sign language at the same time.

Every so often the husband and wife would criticize each other saying, "No, you're wrong. You are using the wrong sign." They would go back and forth. I became confused. Who was right? Then I asked them, "How long have you been married?"

"Oh," they replied, "seven years."

"That's long enough to be able to communicate with each other without any great difficulty," I said. "Why then do you keep on disagreeing about signs? I don't understand."

The wife explained to me the reason why their sign languages were not exactly the same. They came from two different schools. Oh, I could understand then why they sometimes disagreed, especially when the two schools were probably far apart. That would explain why their signs would be that much different. But, no, that was not true. They told me their schools were in the same town and that they were within walking distance of each other. Yet their sign languages were tremendously different. I asked them to explain to me how that happened.

The wife said, "Well, one school was run by nuns for girls only. The other school was run by the Christian Brothers for boys only. For over 150 years the Christian Brothers and the nuns were not on speaking terms. They were not friendly with each other. If they met, they both looked the other way. That explains why their sign languages became increasingly different."

It was really sad. What a shame! Can you imagine how the boys and girls felt when they finished school, met each other, and started to talk, only to find out that they couldn't understand each other? The wife told me that it was not until about four years before that that they finally set up a committee to develop one sign language. They chose a few people to help unify the two different sign languages into one that could be used all over the country. They selected some signs from the girls' school, some signs from the boys' school, and then they modified the signs a little. They put these signs in a book called *The Unified Sign Language*. They published the book and distributed it to the two schools and to other schools in Ireland. Now everyone is happy.

After explaining this the wife asked me, "Do you know what we call this sign language now?"

"No, what?" I asked.

"Unisex Language!" she replied.

Impossible Dream?

Thomas A. Mayes

I grew up in the state of Oregon, way out west. When I was about sixteen years old, I came to Washington, D.C., to attend a Boy Scout Jamboree. It was a wonderful experience for young boys from the farm country. We camped across the Potomac River in an area that I would guess now is the LBJ Memorial Grove. There were several thousand of us there. One day I read in the camp paper that Dr. Percival Hall, President of Gallaudet College, had invited the deaf Scouts to the campus for a picnic and a chance to socialize.

The picnic was on Hotchkiss Field. There were about thirty of us. We had a wonderful time talking and getting to know each other. I also had the opportunity to shake hands and talk with the second president of Gallaudet College.

At that age all of us youngsters had big aspirations for ourselves. I asked Dr. Hall if it was possible for a deaf person to earn a doctorate degree. Dr. Hall, instead of asking why not, which is the appropriate thing to say these days, asked why. He said it was hard enough for deaf people to get a B.A. degree.

Gallaudet and I

Nancy Rarus

When the doctor told me that my baby was deaf, I looked at my son and made the letter "A." The baby was just crawling, but in my mind a vision unfolded—a vision in the past of a man named Thomas Hopkins Gallaudet and a little girl named Alice. Alice was a small deaf girl who had never been to school. Many years ago there were no schools for deaf children. Families often locked them in mental institutions, and hid them away in shame. Gallaudet, who was a minister, was walking along one day when he saw the little girl playing. He had heard talk among the neighbors that something was wrong with her. She was deaf. He tapped Alice on the shoulder, and she looked up at him. Mr. Gallaudet wanted to help her. He taught her how to write the word, h-a-t. This was her first word, *hat*! Alice was excited; she ran to her father, a rich doctor.

The doctor noticed Gallaudet's real interest in Alice and her deafness. Friends and rich neighbors of the doctor in Hartford, Connecticut, talked among themselves and decided to send Thomas Gallaudet to England. This was back around 1815. They had heard that there was a school for deaf people in England. Perhaps Gallaudet could learn how to set up such a school in the United States for Alice and others who were deaf.

Mr. Gallaudet went to England, but he got nothing there, no help at all. When he asked why the teachers would not tell him anything, they said that their method of teaching the deaf was a family secret. He went on to Scotland, but he received the same answer. Teachers wouldn't help him. Gallaudet did learn that students there were not allowed to sign; the teachers slapped their hands if they tried. Speech (oralism) was emphasized. The teachers in Scotland told Gallaudet that he had better go to France.

Thomas Gallaudet went to France and found sign language being used. Do you know how the French people learned sign language? They learned from the priests. In the past, the monks taught the deaf children of very rich families. The monks developed a way to communicate with deaf children in sign language. This method was brought from Italy to France. Gallaudet found a school for the deaf in France which he went to visit.

Abbé Sicard, the head of the school, met Mr. Gallaudet and was very happy to show him how the deaf were taught in the school. He also introduced Gallaudet to Laurent Clerc. Clerc was deaf. "Clerc can show you how to teach the deaf," the Abbé said. So Mr. Gallaudet stayed in France. He learned that Mr. Clerc was a fine man, and he was tempted to steal Clerc away from the school. He did ask Clerc to go to America with him. Mr. Clerc thought about it, and finally Gallaudet convinced him. Abbé Sicard was disappointed, but he agreed to let Clerc go for a short time. However, Laurent Clerc never went back to teach in France again.

Thomas Gallaudet returned to the United States with Clerc. They established a school for the deaf in Hartford, Connecticut, with seven children. One of them was Alice. That happened way back in 1817.

Researchers have learned from some old papers that Alice felt isolated as a deaf child. She felt uncomfortable around hearing people. She felt the same way many deaf people feel today. Once Alice wrote a letter to a friend complaining that her mother forced her to go to tea. "I hate to go to tea, sipping, and watching the hearing ladies gossip," she said. "I feel isolated. I would rather stay home alone; it would be better." It is the same now; it is still true for many deaf people.

Mr. Gallaudet, a hearing man, married a deaf woman named Sophia Fowler. They had several children, several hearing children. Theirs was the first deaf-hearing marriage that is documented. Today, there are many marriages between deaf and hearing people.

Now I look at my son who is deaf. I think of Thomas Gallaudet teaching Alice the letter "A." I begin to teach my son "A."

SUGGESTIONS
FOR
FOLLOW-UP ACTIVITIES

1. Vocabulary

There are many new vocabulary words found in the stories. The following vocabulary words have been chosen from all thirty-seven stories. Have the students look up the meanings of the words and then, have them write sentences using the words appropriately.

acclamation	envy	nominate
allowance	exasperation	nonchalantly
astronaut	exhilarating	nonplussed
barnstorm	exile	paralyzed
bilingual	fantasize	semaphore
chaotic	foreman	sketch
commercial (adj)	gesundheit	sociolinguistics
crestfallen	letdown	soundtrack
discrimination	liaison	uproar
eaves	mime	weightlessness
eavesdropper	motion sickness	

2. Idioms and Expressions

The following idioms and expressions are a sample of those found in the stories. Have the students try to define these phrases from the context of the story. This can be done in a class discussion or individually.

work like a horse	pick someone's brain
pitch hay	mother institution
run of the play	take off like a shot
the Big Top	I can't do that to save my life
perk up	fit into a mold
mustered up his courage	mental crutch
blockhead	a family secret
not helping the situation	the tables are turned

3. Compositions and Stories

The following are suggestions for written compositions or stories that can be told in class.

- describe a summer job, or an experience at summer camp
- describe a scary situation
- describe a dream or fantasy that seemed real
- think of some word games to help remember information, i.e., h-o-m-e-s for the Great Lakes
- describe a funny incident that happened with a brother/sister
- describe a pet, real or imagined
- think of some things that hearing people think deaf people can't do, that they really can do
- describe the first time you were allowed to go out by yourself
- write a story that teaches a lesson, or has a moral
- write about your goals and aspirations for the future

4. Group Projects

Have the students begin a deaf heritage project to find out the history of deaf people in either their home towns or the town where the school is located. The project could result in a newsletter or deaf heritage album to add to the school's library collection.*

Have the students interview deaf adults in the community to find out what it was like to grow up deaf, to find out how their school has or hasn't changed, and to find out how community services have changed over the years.

Have the students collect stories and anecdotes from deaf adults. If video tape equipment is available, tape the students or adults telling these stories. If the equipment is not available, have the students or adults present the stories at an assembly program or in a class.

---

*The students may want to refer to "The World Around You" (published by Pre-College Programs at Gallaudet College) as an example of a student newsletter; and *Deaf Heritage*, by Jack R. Gannon, as an example of an album.